HOME BASE

Marriage

Essentials for a Healthy Marriage
That Will Last Through the Generations

LEOP▲RD
Home Base Ministries

E D D I E   A N D   D A W N   L E O P A R D

Contents

Introduction

Allow us to introduce ourselves and tell how we introduced ourselves to each other.

We met on a football field in August in Columbia, South Carolina. It was just weeks before the college football season started. I (Eddie) played for the University of South Carolina and so I was out jogging around the stadium before practice, and I (Dawn) was in town with my family, moving my brother into college. We drove out to the stadium to look around, and we got a lot more than we bargained for.

We were the only ones there, and Eddie was the only player out there jogging. He got cuter the closer he got to us. However, our first conversation (actually it was not even much of a conversation) did not go well. It ended with me thinking he was an arrogant, egotistical jock who only deserved my best eye roll and nothing else. But, after one more lap around the track, he stopped for a real conversation, and I was smitten. He really was as sweet as he was cute, and, a few weeks later, at the age of seventeen, sitting in the stands at a game, I told my mom, "I'm going to marry him one day."

EDDIE

Many colleges claim to have the best game day entrance in

college football. The University of South Carolina is one of them. That is where I met Dawn, right where the team enters the playing field before all their home games. Years later, when we would attend some of the games, I would always tell our four children, "Right down there is where I met your mom." When they got some age on them, before every game, as the team gathered at that spot to enter the playing field, one of our four would say, "Yeah, Dad, we know, that is where you met Mom." I think it was a divinely inspired meeting. I seldom, if ever, jogged around the field before practice. I have no idea why I did so that day, other than to meet the woman of my dreams, even though she was only sixteen (I know she says she was seventeen). And yes, I was arrogant.

DAWN

Okay, maybe I lied. Maybe I was only sixteen, but I was close to seventeen, and at that age you always count up. We did not actually meet again until December, when our family went to the Gator Bowl. This time it was in a lobby of the hotel where the team was staying. Again, the meeting was short and sweet. My dad was quick to remind me that Eddie was at least five years older, and we left.

A month later, we were dating. I was seventeen by then. Two years and seven months after that, we were married, and the rest, as they say, is history.

Our dating was long and long-distance. I was still in high school, and my parents insisted that I finish, like good parents would. We lived two hours apart from each other. We took turns on the weekend traveling to each other's homes. His parents graciously let me stay with them during visits, and my parents did the same for Eddie. My dad had to practice being gracious and hospitable until he was convinced that Eddie was not that egotistical player (and player in more ways than one) that I thought he was at first. It did not take Dad long. I will not say they were instant friends, but before long they were great friends. It does not take Eddie long to win anyone over. For me, it just took one more lap around the stadium.

EDDIE

During this time, I had actually finished my playing eligibility with football, but I took a class at school so that I could play baseball the following spring. I also was trying out for some NFL teams and went away to training camp in New York. The time away, the long-distance dating, was not easy, but it served us well. Our dating relationship was definitely unconventional, but so much of our life, ministry, and how we did family has been unconventional, as well. Maybe God was getting us ready for a lifelong adventure of the unconventional.

As of today, we have been married for thirty-six years. We have four grown children who all married extremely well and have blessed us with six grandchildren — so far. Life has been an amazing journey. Some days were harder than others. Some seasons were more difficult. This journey has allowed us to minister in some great churches and to many people along the way. God has let us cross paths with some amazing people.

We have worked hard and are still working to have a healthy marriage. And now we try to give back, whether by sharing what we did that worked or did not work, moments of success, or times of blowing it. And that is what this book is about. It is the purpose behind it.

DAWN

God has been good. He has graced us more than we deserve and redeemed so many decisions we made and actions we took that could have taken us under. We owe Him everything. We are so far from perfect, but we serve a perfect God. He has taken so many of our blunders and made them beautiful, as only He could do. We definitely were the unconventional pastor's family. We did so many things differently than what probably most thought we should have or assumed we did. Some of that was out of ignorance, and some of it was just in search of a better, more transparent way of life that we both longed for. I pray that is in no way offensive to you.

We are blessed to live close to our grownup children and grands. It is one of the ways God has blessed us. What a joy it is to see them raising their children and the next generation to love and serve Jesus and to love people along the way. What more could we ask for?

So that is us in a nutshell. Hopefully, when you read the last page, you will feel like you know us or know us better, as it is our desire to be transparent on each page. Every story is different. Yours does not have to look like ours. How boring would the world be if we were all the same?

We are also pleased to introduce you to our four children and their spouses, and we are thrilled that each couple agreed to share parts of their marriage story with you in these pages.

Chrissie Hux is our firstborn. She and her husband, Michael, are the parents of our three precious grand-girls, Brooklynn, Mackenzie and Addison. Michael is the student pastor at our church, Fairview, and Chrissie is a stay-at-home mom who runs a business online.

Jessica Broome is our daughter and second-born child. She and her husband, Justin, are the parents of two of our grand-buddies, Ezra and Jed. Justin is the volunteer coordinator for Miracle Hill Ministries, and Jessica is the adoption coordinator for Quiver Full Adoptions Inc., a private domestic adoption agency. They make their home in the Upstate of South Carolina and attend NewSpring Church.

Stephen is our third child and firstborn son. He is married to Kaylin, who is the event coordinator for Miracle Hill Ministries. Stephen is pastor of Dunean Church in Greenville, South Carolina. They are expecting their first child in the fall of 2021.

John is our fourth child. He is married to Noelle, and together they have another one of our grand-buddies, Jaxon. They live in the Upstate of South Carolina, as well. They are both employed by NFM Lending. Noelle is a loan processor, and John is a loan officer assistant. Their church home is Hope Church.

Chapter One

There is a method to the madness.

"I knew exactly what to do, but in a much more real sense I had no idea what to do." — The Office

DAWN

"Lord, we thank you that you have brought _____ and _____ together. We believe it is by your divine providence. Bless this husband as protector and provider. Bless this wife. Give her the tenderness that will make her great, the inner beauty that never fails. Give them both a deep sense of understanding and a great faith in Thee. Give them a great spiritual purpose in life. May they seek Your kingdom, O Lord. May they not expect perfection of each other; that belongs to Thee alone."

This is part of a prayer Eddie has prayed over many, many couples at the end of the wedding ceremony. As we start our first book on marriage, it seems appropriate to begin with this prayer. This is our prayer for every married couple. It is a prayer for ourselves. It is a blessing on the husband and wife. It is a prayer that their focus would be on God's kingdom and not their own. It is a warning against a few things that can get in our way, things like impossible expectations.

Writing a book on marriage seemed like a good idea, even a God idea, when Eddie and I first felt the prodding. But, honestly, as I sit here staring at a blank screen, the only thing I feel is overwhelmed, unqualified and downright intimidated, to the point of anxiety-driven fear. And here is why:

Other than talking about Jesus, marriage is my favorite topic to talk about, read about, think about. It is the first institution God ordained — yes, even before the church, and definitely before government.

But when you do something like this, you set yourself up for several things. One: People tend to think that either your marriage is perfect or that you think it is. I do not know how to scream this any louder: Our marriage is far from perfect! It never has been perfect, and it never will be. As a matter of fact, no one's marriage is perfect, no matter how much they would like for you to believe it is. We have never spent a half-second of one day thinking that ours is a model, or *the* model. It is good. In fact, it is great! But we have worked dang hard, and we still do, in all the areas that we will discuss in this book, to have a healthy, thriving marriage.

We are just two people who, by the grace of God, have been married for a while now and we can share with others a few things we did right and some things we did wrong (that, hopefully, you can avoid). God has redeemed an awful lot on our behalf.

Two: There are people who claim that times are different and people are different, so what worked then will not work now. I know that times have changed to some degree. I tend to believe people have changed more than the times. People are focused on different things and may live at a faster pace. Maybe so. However, people are people. We have issues, problems and struggles now, just like we always have. Maybe they come dressed in a different package, but most are the same. One thing that has not changed is God. He is the same yesterday, today and forever. I do not know if you are a person of faith or if a belief in God is part of your life, but our belief is that God is the One who created marriage and all its goodness, and He is the One who knows how to take two very imperfect people, bring them together, and make something good, something very good, from it. His handbook still works. And doing marriage His way worked in days past, it works now, and it will work in the future.

Marriage does not have to be perfect to be good — yes, even great. In fact, it never will be perfect. That is part of the great adventure of a lifelong love in the form of marriage.

Our desire is for others to realize that a marriage based on the principles of God's Word works.

EDDIE

John and Sally met on a dating service, and it seemed to click. They dated for a while, had a short engagement, and then got married. Many of their friends were living together, but they were more traditional. Both were involved in church and even had a church wedding. It was good. They both had jobs they loved and were in love with each other. Three years into marriage they had their first child, just like they had planned. Sally focused on being a mom and John focused more on his job. In fact, he was working long hours, even on weekends. They were exhausted. They had a nice home and two new cars, but the marriage was strained. Several years passed and they had another child. Sally says John is not the same man she married. John says Sally has let herself go and is more interested in being a mom than a wife. So they separate. And while separated, they both hook up with old flames on social media and start new relationships.

Now, I made up that story. John and Sally are not real people. But you could change the names, and many people would say, that is me, that is us, been there done that, or that is where I am right now.

DAWN

Marriage is hard work, friends! I am not sure why people think you will not have to work at it just because you love each other. If anyone has ever told you that marriage is easy, they either lied to you, or they have forgotten. Let me just say, "I'm sorry," on their behalf.

How can dying to self and serving someone else, putting their needs ahead of your own, all while you have different love languages and different styles of relating, different temperaments and personalities, be easy? Yet God puts us under one roof, adds a few other little selfish, needy bodies to the home and says, "Husbands, love your wives like I love the church," and "Wives, submit yourselves to your husbands."

Sound easy to you? Yeah, glad I am not alone. That is why so often I find myself wanting to say, when someone is grumbling about marriage being hard, "What exactly did you expect it to be like?"

Great would be a word I would use to describe my marriage, but never easy. Adventurous? Yes! Rollercoaster ride? Yes! But not easy.

We had four little ones. That is six selfish, needy people under one roof. At one time their ages were six, three, nineteen months and newborn. In case you need help with the math, two were fifteen months apart, and then two were nineteen months apart. And yes, we figured it out. We did not stop, but we got smart — after the scare of a fifth one.

And then, you guessed it, four little ones that close in age turned into four teenagers at one time. Under one roof.

On top of that, my husband pastored a large church and traveled to conferences, conventions and speaking engagements. He traveled the world with groups, usually ten days to two weeks at a time. And I stayed home to be a full-time mom.

There were times Eddie would come home and I would go outside or down the street just to have thirty minutes to myself without having to answer a question, referee an argument, change a diaper, feed a mouth or be on the receiving end of another request.

Were there times I would be curled up in a fetal position? Yes.

Were there times I would be way out on a ledge, desperate

for time and attention from my husband? Yes.

Were there times I could have used more help from him? Yes.

Were there times I was jealous of a church full of people needing time and attention from my husband? Yes.

Ministry is a never-ending cycle of needs and demands. I had pity parties in my head and my heart that would often spill out after being suppressed for lengthy periods. That is never pretty. "He is spending all his time with other people. He is meeting all their needs. He is not here spending time with me or meeting my needs." Classic.

Am I complaining? No, not really. I have loved our life. I have loved raising a family. I have loved ministry. But what I am saying, again, is that it does not have to be easy to be good. We have had, and do have, an amazing life. I would not trade with anyone! Life is not easy for anyone. Marriage is not easy for anyone.

We moved places where, on the front end, I did not really want to go.

We lived places where I felt terribly alone.

We have had times of sitting across the table from each other asking the hard questions, saying the hard things.

We have tabled arguments and whispered our way through them so young ears did not hear.

We have fought over money.

We have fought for alone time.

We have fought for our own way.

We have fought to be heard and understood.

But the biggest fight we have ever had, we fought together. That is the fight to not give up, to not quit, to forgive, to know it is worth it to persevere, to know it will not be better somewhere else, with someone else.

You just do it. And you keep doing it. You keep choosing one another like you vowed to do.

EDDIE

I am deeply concerned. I am not the most positive person in the world, according to my wife. I consider myself a realist. Norman Vincent Peale, I am not.

But what I read, hear, and see tells me we are in big trouble as far as traditional marriage is concerned. What has happened to the institution of marriage — one man and one woman committed to one another in the eyes of God for a lifetime?

A study conducted by Rutgers University, "The National Marriage Project," revealed that Americans have not forsaken marriage, but there has been a significant decline since 1960 in the number of couples who actually marry. Over the last five decades Americans have become less likely to marry, and of those who do marry, fewer consider their marriages to be happy marriages. The divorce rate is more than twice that of 1960, and the number of couples living together has increased dramatically over the past five decades.[1]

Mark Driscoll cited a New York Times article. In 1996, 2.9 million couples were co-habitant in the U.S. In 2012, that number was 7.8 million, or an increase of almost 170 percent.[2]

It is obvious that Americans live longer, marry later, divorce sooner and choose to live together outside of marriage — before, after and in-between marriage.

So, with all that negativity stated, let me be positive. There are many couples who have been married many years, and they are very happy, very fulfilled and very much in love — in fact, more in love than ever. Struggles, yes. Issues, yes. Disagreements, yes. Those things happen in every marriage. Men, your wife will not always please you. Ladies, your husband will not always be all you expected him to be. There will be stormy seas and rocky roads, but there can also be unending love and lasting commitment. And it is true that you can love someone even more the longer you are married than you did on your wedding day — more than you ever thought possible.

DAWN

We talk, and we hear people talk, about how "the times have changed." One of the changes I have noticed is that we are a much softer people. We are an entitled people. We actually believe marriage is about our happiness, when it is really about our holiness. We give up on things way too quickly. Where is the fight, the drive, the competitiveness to push through, to roll up our sleeves and work through the mess that, many times, we created? When I was young, my parents never let us quit anything until it was over. I had to finish the year or finish the season. We raised our children the same way. At the end of a year or season, it is a good time to reevaluate to see if you want to continue something. I am talking extracurricular activities and sports, by the way, not school. But, once you start something, that is it. Letting your team down, wasting time and money, is not an option. "Just suck it up and finish" was the philosophy under the Leopard roof. But time and time again we saw kids being allowed to quit halfway through for all kinds of reasons. "The coach is mean." "She does not like me." "I am tired of it." "I don't like it anymore." "I don't get enough playing time." And on and on the excuses go. We create a monster mentality that says when life is tough, just quit. When things get hard, then move on. And we see people do that in marriage, in jobs, in church. We just move from one to another to another.

Please know that none of this pertains to those in abusive situations. That is totally different. We are talking instead about the petty differences that grow because we do not communicate, or because we just want our way in every situation.

We are talking about bitter roots that take hold and grow deep because we refuse to let go and don't choose to forgive. We just "aren't in love with them anymore or attracted to them anymore," or, "I just cannot stand the way ...." And we give up, maybe right before the blessing or the breakthrough. We do not think we should have to work at it if we really love each other. That is the brilliance of middle school or high school maturity and mindset. In reality we just want someone new, someone different.

Truth is, bad times come for us all. It rains on the just and the unjust. Issues are unavoidable.

There are a few things I believe can help.

As simple as it sounds, laugh a little — preferably, a lot. That seems like a hard task when you feel like it is all you can do to keep your head above water, but as Scripture tells us in Proverbs, a cheerful heart is good medicine. Science even tells us that we all need thirty minutes of exercise three times a week, and we need fifteen minutes of laughter each day. There has to be something we can find in the madness to laugh about. It may take some searching, but it is worth it.

Another thing that helps is faith. Faith really will get us through times we never thought we could survive. When times have been the toughest in my life, I went back to the place where I knew God was trustworthy. If we are followers of Jesus, we are called to embrace all His teaching. He not only taught us, but showed us, how to love and how to forgive. And those are two things we will have to embrace over and over if we want a strong, healthy, life-giving, long-lasting marriage. We will overlook the petty things that annoy us and we will forgive the big things that have the capacity to kill us if we choose to let them. Yes, it is a choice. God never promised us an easy road as individuals or married couples. Another misconception people have is that life as a believer will be smooth and easy. But He did promise to be with us, and with Him we can do all things.

Finally, I would say, remember. Remember what it was like when you met. This may be a stretch, but my guess is you would not have gotten married if you had not loved each other in some way. Sometimes the everyday stuff just clouds our memory. It clouds our thinking. The issues and problems make us wonder why we ever stepped into this to begin with. Remembering helps. Satan's role is to cause us to focus on the bad and forget the good. He messes with our minds. One of the roles of the Holy Spirit is to cause us to remember. Ask Him to remind you of the good things that the pressures of life have stolen.

Ask Him to remind you of the reasons and purpose behind beginning this journey together. And ask Him to remind you of all that God has already brought you through as individuals and as a couple.

He will be faithful and do that.

I love Numbers 16 in the Bible. Have you ever read that passage? Numbers 16 teaches us that the road to destruction starts with dissatisfaction. We exaggerate our problems. We long for something better, and instead of making what we already have better, we go looking elsewhere. Korah, in his ambition for more, lost everything. And that is what many of us do. In our longing for better and more, we lose everything — our spouse, our children, our home, our job, our very life. In a different, but similar way, we, like Korah, get swallowed up. God is still in the resurrection business. The resurrection changes things. It brings life to dead things. It changes circumstances that seem dire and without hope.

There is no marriage too far gone for God to resurrect. If only we would stop looking around, and look up.

EDDIE

Let's look closely at the institution of marriage.

In Genesis 1 we see six times that God observed His creation and said, "It is good!" In fact, the last verse of chapter 1, verse 31, says God saw all that He had made and it was "very good" (NIV). But then suddenly in Genesis 2:18 God said, "It is not good." It is not good for the man to be alone. So, in 2:18b, God declares that He will make Adam a helper.

Now, I know that some women have looked at this passage and have said what God meant is, "I can do better than this; I'll make an upgrade."

Some men have looked at this and said that God made beast and man and then rested, and then He made woman — and since then neither God, beast, nor man have rested.

But those views are not biblical, and we want to stick with a biblical view of marriage.

What we see here is that marriage was God's idea, and because it was God's idea, it was a good idea. What God is saying is that man is not complete — you need help — so He created a helper. The word helper is a bigger word. It means completer/partner.

So God put Adam to sleep, took a rib from his side, and made a woman. A Jewish rabbi once commented on this, and I often quote this at weddings. He said God took the rib because it was from under Adam's arm so that he could protect her, close to his heart so that he could love her, and from his side so that she could walk beside him in equality all through life. God did not take a bone from Adam's hand that he might use her as a tool, nor from his foot that he might walk over her, nor from his head that she would walk over him (or from his neck that she would be a pain in the neck). God took the rib so they could walk side by side throughout life. She would complete him and complement him, and he would complement her.

Do not miss Adam's response. We miss so much of the emotion on the printed page. Adam did not wake up, yawn, and, in a slow drawl, say, "Bone of my bone and flesh of my flesh." God had created a beautiful partner who was just right for him. There was excitement and emotion. The Living Bible says, "This is it!" Adam recognized immediately that she was the one.

Since God created marriage, then He must know what is best for marriage and what makes it work.

Three things are vital: Leave, Cleave, and Become One.

Leave

Leave means to turn away from, or break away from. Simply put, when you get married you leave your parents. That is the subtle aspect of the wedding ceremony that we miss if we are not careful. There is a public commitment to one another and a goodbye to parents. This does not mean you stop honoring or loving your parents. But there is a new relationship now that takes priority. There are moms who will not let go of their adult children. There are dads who think they know best. And there are married children who continue running home every time they have a fuss.

We had that problem with my mom. She was always quick with advice and demands that would require my time and shift my focus away from my marriage. I considered sitting down and talking to her, but a wise mentor suggested a letter. That way, instead of constantly having to sit down and talk, I could remind her to read the letter again.

Cleave

"Bond" is another word for cleave. It means super-glue. It means totally together. Again, this is part of the wedding ceremony. It says, "Forsaking all others, I choose you." And it means we continue to choose one another every single day. But an issue that arises today comes from our easy access to social media. We get on Facebook. We open Instagram. We have lunch with someone from work, and we begin to share and commiserate, when the safest thing to do is burn some bridges, bomb some canyons, and stop commiserating with others and consoling others. It leads us to bond with the wrong people in the wrong places. If you need to vent and commiserate over your home life, do that in the safety net of biblical counseling. Preferably you go to counseling with your spouse, but if not, at least that is a safe place for you. Talking and sharing personal issues with anyone other than your spouse, especially someone of the opposite sex, is very dangerous. Do not think Satan won't gain a foothold there.

Another place our bonding is out of order is with our children. No one loves her children more than my wife, but she bonded to me. Children should be a close second, but your spouse comes first. Too often, bonding with our children creates a problem when they grow up and leave, and we find ourselves in the empty nest. You are strangers to one another. Dawn and I loved and supported our children, and we surely did a lot of things wrong, but that is one thing we did right. An empty nest is great when you have spent years bonding to one another.

Do not cleave to your career, either. Be ambitious, provide for your family, be a leader, but do not neglect your family. We will talk more about this, but just know, in case you do not, cleaving to a career can leave you cold and alone in your later years if you do not have the proper perspective of work.

Become One

This is the miracle of marriage. Some say, "We understand the two are to become one — we just can't decide which one." Too often the wife is totally in love with her husband and he is totally in love with himself, or vice versa.

Part of becoming one flesh is what happens in private after the ceremony, but it is so much more than the physical/sexual relationship. We want to be one socially, emotionally, and spiritually. Souls are meant to fit together just as our bodies do. Take walks together, spend time together. Put the phone down and talk.

We want you to hear from Michael and Chrissie. They set some things up and found out some things early in their marriage.

Michael and Chrissie: After ten years of marriage, we thought we would be more prepared to chat on the topic of marriage than we are now. Honestly, we're very much still trying to figure this whole thing out. However, there are a few things that we believe have given our marriage a firm backbone.

Now, before I (Chrissie) jump in, there's something you need to know about me. I have a passion — a deep-deep passion: lists. I'm an avid list-maker. I have them everywhere. It's how I function on a daily basis. So, saying that, I think the only logical way for me to break down some things for you is via a list. Hope that's okay!

Date Nights

Chrissie: Michael and I didn't really date before we got married. No, it wasn't an arranged marriage or anything like that. He lived in Florida and I lived in South Carolina. So we dated via Skype. (For you Generation Z-ers, that's the same thing as FaceTime.) Long story short, we saw each other a few times a year, and then we got married. So, when we got married, Michael was insistent upon having a weekly date night. I assumed he was just trying to make up for lost time (haha), but I went with it. I can tell you that we have probably missed our weekly date night maybe three times in the last ten years. And because we set that standard at the beginning of our marriage, it made it so much easier once children came along to continue to make it non-negotiable. I'm so very thankful that Michael makes it a priority now because everyone knows Mama needs a break at least once a week. I can honestly say that it not only makes me a better wife, but also a better mom.

Michael: From day one, if there was one thing that was going to be a non-negotiable, it was date night. I wanted Chrissie to know she was a priority. I wanted her to look forward to a night each week so that we could connect, and for her to continue to feel pursued. If you want your wife to still feel pursued, have a date night once a week. I also wanted our children to see us making our marriage a priority, because great marriage makes great parents.

Self-Care

Chrissie: Okay, now I know I just got some eye-rolls with this item on my list, and whether you think this topic is biblical or not, I pray you hear me out. At the beginning of our marriage, I was around a group of women who had the mindset of, "My husband married me for me; I don't need to worry about my physical appearance." Basically, *he married me, so he's stuck with me.* That conversation was in response to a speaker we were listening to who said it was important to her that she got completely "dolled-up" before her husband left the house for work in the mornings. She wanted him to leave the house with her best self on his mind. While I don't necessarily fall on either one of those sides of the spectrum (because I can rock leggings and a mom-bun with the best of them), I do think it's important that we care for ourselves. I think it's important that we pull ourselves together daily. That may look different for you than it does for me, but I've found that changing out of my PJs (even when I don't want to), throwing on some moisturizer (and mascara if I'm feeling fancy), and brushing my hair (or throwing it in my famous mom-bun) does wonders for my spirit. On a more spiritual note, I've noticed that unless I've taken care of my body and my soul, I'm a hot mess. I can always trace my bad attitude and bad decisions back to not taking proper care of my body and/or my heart. Jesus retreated alone multiple times to take care of his soul. I think we can all learn something from that. After all, we cannot pour from an empty cup, and if I'm going to pour out onto my husband and kids all day long, I have to be pouring from a cup that's been filled. So maybe the term "self-care" rubs you the wrong way and you would be more comfortable using the term "soul care." Either way, we have found that taking care of our mind, body, and spirit has been so beneficial for our marriage.

Michael: How can I lead in our marriage if I am not taking care of myself? If I'm not healthy, how can I love my wife or my kids to the fullest? How can we even love God with all our strength if we aren't taking care of ourselves?

The biggest thing I can do in order for us to have a healthy marriage is to spend time with Jesus. A right relationship with my spouse is determined by a right relationship with God. Whenever my time with God has lacked, so has my marriage.

Love Languages

Chrissie: Whenever people used to talk about love languages, I would privately roll my eyes. Yeah, I knew it was important, but I felt like all the love languages were important. I was always conflicted because I didn't want Michael to only buy me gifts or spend time with me "because he had to" in order to make me feel loved. I wanted him to do them out of the goodness of his heart. I know I'm not alone in this, right, ladies? Pre-kids, my love language was Gifts and Quality Time. Once we had kids, I'm pretty sure my love language quickly switched to *Acts of Service* (aka: help me with these kids). (Okay, maybe not completely switched, but they're definitely at a tie.) By the way, if you don't know your spouse's love language, I recommend figuring it out! A lot of our issues in marriage have been because we (okay, I) haven't been intentional enough with this. His love languages are Words of Affirmation & Physical Touch. Do you want to know where Words of Affirmation & Physical Touch rank on my spectrum? The very, very bottom. Like, the very last two. Funny how that always works, eh? I've had to work super hard at affirming him. It's totally not my jam, but it's what he needs from me. It's what makes him feel respected. At the end of the day, I'll write you a letter, but opening up my mouth and using words is difficult for me. (Hello, my name is Chrissie and I'm an introvert.) However, a lot of our disagreements could have been avoided if I had simply opened my mouth and said, "I'm proud of you for that" or "Great job!" In my defense, though, adding children to the mix has made this way harder. I've struggled a lot with switching from mom mode, which I'm in all day, to wife mode. I affirm my kids all day long and I also try to show them physical affection all day long, so when Michael walks in the door from work, I'm done affirming and definitely don't want to be touched! I'm sure you'll slowly start to realize that when you act outside of your love language to meet your spouse's love language, it can be exhausting — but it's worth it.

Michael: It took me almost three years to learn Chrissie's love language. After pouring my heart into a card for her birthday one year and hardly getting a reaction at all, I quickly learned that Words of Affirmation was not her love language. I was loving her in our early years like I wanted to be loved, when her love language was Gifts and Quality Time. Once I discovered her love language, I was able to flourish in our marriage and make her feel the most loved. Taking Gary Chapman's test online can truly allow you to love your spouse to the fullest.

Heart Issues/Conclusion

In a counseling session we had before getting married, Dr. Bernie Cueto told us that issues in marriage are like issues in a car. Sometimes a light on your dashboard will come on as a warning that something might be wrong under the hood. It's a signal that you may want to have something checked out before a bigger issue arises. We try to always recognize when those lights turn on and address it then. A lot of what we have discovered about marriage revolves around the placement of our heart. When we are having "off days" in our marriage, nine times out of ten it's a heart issue within ourselves that we can settle between ourselves and the Lord.

EDDIE

The truth is, I do not care how romantic or faithful you are, if Jesus is not the foundation of your marriage, it will never be all that God intends for it to be.

I have yet to meet a person who said that they established their marriage on biblical principles, followed God's plan, and it failed. Of course, there are still challenges and setbacks. We are a self-centered people. The lie is that it should be easy. We have to be intentional. But God's way works.

"People call these imperfections, but no, that's the good stuff. Then we get to choose who we let into our weird little worlds. You're not perfect, sport, and let me save you the suspense. This girl you met? She isn't perfect, either. But the question is whether or not you're perfect for each other. That's the whole deal. That's what intimacy is all about." — Sean Maguire, Good Will Hunting

Chapter Two

Back to back …
Not nose to nose …
Fighters ready?

"It's like I used to tell my wife, I do not apologize unless I think I'm wrong, and if you don't like it you can leave. And I say the same thing to my current wife, and I'll say it to my next one, too."
— The Office

D A W N

Anyone like to watch a good fight? The men in our family love it when one of the big fights comes on, and they will sometimes pay money to watch them. A few years ago, Eddie passed on going to his fortieth high school reunion so that he and the guys in our family could watch a big fight together. Sometimes they can even make a big event out of it. They may invite a bunch of people over or go to a local place to be with a big group to watch the fight together. What about the hockey fights? Do we not all love to go watch a hockey match, secretly hoping the players will have one good fight before it is over? And the baseball brawl! Who can resist getting excited when the batter charges the pitcher's mound? Well, maybe not this baseball pitcher's mom, but yes, even I, when it does not involve my boys. The benches empty and we all cheer. Why is that? Why do we love that so much? Why does it make our hearts pound and our adrenaline rush? We watch the cat fights and all the drama on reality television and laugh about it, or shake our heads. The sad thing about that is that it does not really surprise us. Why? Because we know that so often that is how we all act.

Bottom line is that sometimes, maybe a lot of times, people are just mean. The title "mean girls" is justified, and not necessarily for the young middle school, high school age. I have known some mean girls who have long since left high school. Some fashion and home décor bloggers I follow have said how many mean direct messages they get from people, how critical and hateful people can be. And we are talking fashion and décor, friends! I can tell you that some of the meanest emails we have received have come from people in our church. And do not get me started on the anonymous letters we have received. Letters criticizing everything from the structure of the church, to a program that has been cut because it is no longer effective, to the way I dress, or telling us they wish our entire family would leave the area. Mean girls (and boys) grow up, and unfortunately they get meaner with age. Please do not let that shock you, friends, or discourage you from attending a local church. Mean people are everywhere, including church. We have been their targets, and many of you have been, as well.

Let's have a quick science class. If you are not into science stuff, feel free to jump ahead, but this is so interesting. When we get angry, the body's heart rate, arterial tension and testosterone production increases, cortisol (the stress hormone) decreases, and the left hemisphere of the brain becomes more stimulated. When we get mad, our rational prefrontal lobes shut down, and the reflexive back areas of the brain take over. A tense body pumps out cholesterol, and a group of chemicals called catecholamines encourage fatty deposits to pile up in the heart and carotid arteries. It is no shock that angry people are three times more likely to have a heart attack than those less prone to fury. Stress can increase stomach acids. Anger causes a surge in the stress hormone cortisol, which bumps up oil production and leads to acne and other skin problems. It also affects the nervous system. The nervous system becomes highly activated, making it difficult to return to a relaxed state, which can affect the immune system. Anger ain't pretty, people.

Feelings of anger arise in response to how we interpret and react to certain situations. Everyone has their own triggers, but some are common to most of us: things like feeling threatened or attacked, or people not respecting our feelings or possessions. Some are quick to blame others when they are angry, and some are easily angered when they are already experiencing feelings such as hunger, stress, nervousness, or sadness.

Ever heard the saying or seen the bumper sticker that says, "I'm sorry for what I said when I was hungry"?

Sometimes it can be that simple — sometimes, not so much. One of our sons, from the time he was very little, would become what we called "hangry." That would be the sickness of getting extremely angry when you experience hunger. I am not sure if that is in the latest science books or not, but it is a real thing. No lie, I kept snacks on me all the time just for him. Well, actually, it was for all our benefit so that we would not have to be victims of his hanger. He would just get so angry when those hunger pains would hit. Maybe he still does. Thankfully, I have not witnessed it in a while.

As a matter of fact, I heard on the radio just the other day that most arguments in marriage start due to one or both being hungry. Again, I do not know if that is a scientific fact, but I would not argue that point.

EDDIE

We all must have the mindset that marriage is about we, not me. I am a competitive person, always have been. But it is an important thing that we do not compete with our spouse. The only competition we need in marriage is the competition to out-serve one another. We all have this image in our head of what life looks like, and it never seems to allow for conflict. Conflict is not necessarily bad; it can be healthy. No one agrees on everything, and we shouldn't. Conflict allows for growth. When a husband and a wife both believe that the other one loves them, respects them and is committed to them, it is easier to overlook minor issues, have conversations about major issues, and press forward together. Now, what is minor to one may be major to the other, so do not overlook that and do not make light of things that your spouse considers major just because you see it as minor. A good thing to keep in mind is that not everyone thinks like you or sees things the way you do. There are all kinds of things that can cause conflict and times of discontent — from raising children, to meeting budget, to careers and in-laws, to moves and midlife crises. When stress rises, energy decreases, health issues come along, and in the midst of all of that, huge decisions have to be made. It can create friction. It would be nice if we could stop the clock and just deal with our stuff, but unfortunately life continues to march on. Just let our aim be to fight with each other, for each other, as we strive together for that healthy place. Maybe the best time for conversations, and which may actually help pre-empt arguments, is during peace times. Ask questions. Ask how cared for do you feel. Ask if there is a way you can relieve some stress from your wife/husband. Ask if you have offended your spouse in some way, or what makes them feel cared for and loved. It is so much easier to sit and talk when there is not a huge problem going on or one or both are not on the defensive. When you ask those questions, do it in humility and out of honesty. Do not get mad when they are honest. Respond and react in humility. And can we agree to avoid blame-shifting? Our culture is so good at blaming others for their actions, their feelings, their shortcomings, everything. Remember Genesis 3:12: "Then the man replied, 'The woman you gave to be with me — she gave me some fruit from the tree and I ate'" (NIV). Yep, we have been doing it from the beginning — blaming God and everyone else. Husbands and wives need to embrace responsibility for how things are going in the marriage. It is never one person's fault when things are less than great. If we go into situations thinking, "Well, if he does this, or if she does that, then I'll …." That attitude will get us nowhere fast. Take some internal inventory of self. James 4:1 says, "What is the source of wars and fights among you? Don't they come from the cravings that are at war within you?" (NIV)

DAWN

We have already mentioned that we all seem to enjoy watching a good fight, but do you enjoy being the one in the fight? Neither Eddie nor I enjoy fighting. It may seem weird to think that anyone does, but I believe some people enjoy being a part of a fight. We have been around people who enjoy it, or at least they seem to enjoy it. We have known couples who seem to thrive on it. They are either in one direction, being crazy about each other, or the opposite, fighting like cats and dogs. One of the things we always heard, and it is biblical, was do not let the sun go down on your wrath. Anyone ever stayed up all night? The bad thing about that is we cannot always come to an agreement right away. And some of us — well, most of us — would do better with a cooling-off period. I admit that I used that as an excuse many times to justify my silent treatment. See, I am not one who explodes. I can, and I have, but that is rare for me. I internalize everything. You can make me cry fairly easily. And I hold onto things. I do not get past things quickly, and I sulk. Eddie, on the other hand, hates the silent treatment. That really makes it wrong for me to respond that way. It was definitely a manipulative tool in my armor at times. He does not blow up often either; he just never sees anything as a big deal and worth fighting over. He says nothing is worth fighting about — conversation, yes; fighting, no. Anyway, we cannot let the silent treatment be an excuse. We do need to talk. We also do need a cooling-off period lest we say things we regret. Words cannot be taken back once the trigger is pulled and they are fired out of our mouths.

So yes, take time to cool down. Take time to think. But then someone has to act. Someone has to take the initiative to sit down and communicate.

Would it shock you if I told you that we recently went through a three-week struggle? Hopefully it does not surprise anyone that we struggle, too. But that it went on for three weeks! Honestly, it was a period that neither of us knew what was going on. I could not pinpoint exactly why I was mad at him. He certainly did not know why I was mad, and he did not know why he was mad, either. We were both stressed. We were both tired. We had stopped communicating, other than "How was work?" "Fine." "How was your day?" "Fine." "What do you want for dinner?" "I don't care." "What do you want?" It is easy to see, looking back, why the dark cloud came over us. Satan is always willing to take the opportunity when we are vulnerable to unleash all kinds of hell onto us. During those three weeks, we just both stayed in what my family used to call the "mullygrubs." Right in the middle of that time I had a speaking engagement. Do you have any idea how difficult it is to stand before a room full of women and talk about living for Jesus when you and your husband are in the middle of a silent, but no less deadly, kind of war with one another? I can tell you, looking back over those three weeks, it still brings tears to my eyes. Even down my cheeks. I have such regret over not dealing with it sooner, regret over the way I treated Eddie over those weeks, regret over wasted time and energy. It took him sitting across the table from me one night at dinner, looking me dead in the eye and saying, "I'm sorry." At that point I do not know if he even knew what he was sorry for, because I had not really even told him why I was mad. But he said he was sorry for letting things go so long, and it was his job as the husband to take time to make things right. He was willing to take the initiative. I cannot even describe in words what that did for me, for us — still does — when I think about it. Those two words led to some deep conversation, tons of tears, more "I'm sorry's," reconciliation and reflecting back, realizing that so much of it was misunderstanding and things evolving in our own heads that were total lies. Yes, Satan was all over it.

So, yes, thirty-plus years later, we are still learning, still growing, still screwing up, still trying to get a handle on this whole marriage thing.

EDDIE

As a pastor I have conducted a lot of weddings. I have done a lot of premarital counseling. I still do it, but it so often seems like a waste of time to do counseling because, once the ring is on the finger and the venue is reserved, the couple is not going to turn back, no matter what you tell them. With the emergence of reality shows and such, marriage is taken lightly, and weddings are blown way out of proportion. Fantasy takes over and thousands of dollars are spent on a dream wedding, with very little thought given to the marriage. It is the Cinderella story of the prince sweeping the young girl off her feet. There is a beautiful wedding that Daddy spends more money than he has for his baby girl's dream to come true.

A husband and wife walk out of the church, out of the venue, or off the mountain with the fantasy of children who will always be so well behaved that there will be no calls from the teacher and straight A's on the report card. No one ever gets sick, the dog never pees on the carpet, there is plenty of money for the cars they want to drive (that never need new tires), a nice home that stays magically clean, and vacations just like the travel agent describes. Do not forget about that daddy who expects his little girl to have everything she wants because she always has, and that mom who expects her little boy to be nurtured and appreciated and, of course, let him do whatever he wants because he always has — and you have disaster waiting to happen when the couple returns from the honeymoon, if not before. Reality hits. Feelings come into play. He really is more frog than prince. And she really is just plain spoiled. Enter anger, selfishness, and jealousy as they continue watching reality TV and romantic movies. Conflict is bound to happen. Conflict that they never expected to happen suddenly becomes the daily habit. She does not know why he is not more like … and he has no idea why she will not ….

Conflict is real, and it happens daily in our country and in our homes. Police will tell you the most dangerous calls to deal with are to try and diffuse domestic disputes. Conflict is not a respecter of persons or economic standing. Young and old, rich and poor, educated or not, all races experience conflict. Adam and Eve were in a perfect environment and had issues. Their children, Cain and Abel, had conflict that led to murder. Opposites attract, but they can also attack.

And those reality shows we keep mentioning? Do not forget that those folks are in the perfect setting, and someone else is footing the bill for fantasy dates and even fantasy suites. And we are left sitting here wondering why we chose him, or why we chose her.

DAWN

Have we mentioned that Eddie and I both hate conflict? Yes, I thought so. We would rather eat our arm off than be in conflict with each other or someone else. It seems pointless, a waste of time and energy. We are both champions at clamming up. Sometimes we can blow up. Blowing up is really rare for both of us, though.

We all have those triggers, though, that can send us in a tailspin. Sometimes we pull those triggers or push those buttons that we know will get a response from our spouse, even a negative response. My trigger always goes off when I feel invisible to Eddie. When I struggle to get his attention or his mind seems elsewhere when I talk, but not when others talk to him. When I start turning it over and over in my mind how he seems to be spending all his time with someone else or everyone else seems to be taking priority. When I feel like he would not notice if I disappeared for a few days, except that dinner would not happen, his laundry would pile up and my side of the bed would be empty. Is it not amazing how one tiny thing can send our minds in all kinds of directions, and before we know it we are all worked up and our spouse has no idea why? It is kind of like when I have a dream, and in my dream Eddie does something that makes me mad and I wake up mad at him over it. He is left wondering where in the world this attitude came from. My triggers have a tendency to send all my insecurities to the front line. I do not know what your triggers are. I do not know what sends you into your shell or causes you to come out guns blazing. But whatever it is, or whatever they are, we have to learn how to deal with them and fight well. And by fighting well I mean fighting with your spouse *for* one another. We are not one another's enemies. We are in it together, and we have to work together.

I remember watching a high school baseball game one night. There was a young man pitching for us, and it was a big game. I remember sitting near a friend who was a former coach, and as our pitcher struggled and the game started getting away from us, the former coach said, "He's going to lose this game. And he's not going to make it as a college player" (which at the time everyone was presuming he would be). I asked him why and he said, "He doesn't have the heart. He doesn't seem to be able to dig deep and want it now that things are not going well. You've got to have more guts than that." Wow! That was a lesson we took to our boys who were coming along as pitchers, and I have to say they may not have been the ace on their team every year, but they had heart, and they had a lot of guts, and they won some big games and they fought back in a lot of games when they did not have their best stuff. By the way, that former coach was right; things happened just as he predicted.

Marriage is so much more important than baseball. And most days it takes a lot of guts, and even more heart. Things will not always go our way. We will not always get our way. Life will be hard. And some days we may just want to throw in the towel. But we have to dig deep. Fights and conflicts will happen if we are married longer than a day. But if we are not committed to one another for the long haul — I mean really committed — at some point we will give up and quit. Because life is hard. Most days are not Instagram worthy. We cannot put a pretty filter on it and make things look beautiful when they are not. If you are a newlywed, life gets hard after the honeymoon and the bills start coming and you can no longer buy everything you want, and you cannot go and do your own thing without running things by someone else. If you have young children, we have always said, little ones have little issues, bigger ones have bigger issues. So life gets hard raising a family. Unfortunately, so many divorces take place when the children are in the tween and teen years because life is especially tough then, and if you are not on the same page and you are not fighting together, those are years when you can be torn apart. And you will throw in the towel. Or you may be the rare one who gets to the empty nest but wonders who that person is lying next to you, because for years it has been all about the children or the career and you would rather start over or be alone than live with this stranger. Or you choose to stay together, but life just is not much fun. Whatever season you are in, trust me: It is worth it to hang in there, fight it through together, hang on even on days when it feels like you are hanging by the skin of your teeth. Get some counseling. Choose forgiveness. Think past today.

If you are not already married, hear from a wise friend of ours. He told us that when he talks to young couples about getting married, one of the things he asks is if there is anything that would ever make you leave that person you are getting ready to marry. So often they will start with, "Well, as long as he is faithful," or "As long as she never cheats." He always sends them away to pray through whether they are truly ready to get married.

The answer needs to be: "Nothing." There are a lot of strong marriages that have survived unfaithfulness. I am not talking about any form of abuse, whether physical, emotional or mental, or living in a dangerous environment. I am just saying that we need to trust a God who can redeem and heal the hurtful things we are capable of doing to one another. He is capable of redeeming the most difficult situations. Do not ever think a situation is beyond God's redemptive hand.

EDDIE

I admit it. I am not good at noticing things, especially details. I remember when Dawn was complaining one day that I never seemed to notice what she was wearing or how she looked. My response was, "Well, I would notice if you went out wearing nothing." Not a good comment, fellas.

A man was bragging to his friends about a fight he had with his wife. He told them at one point that she came crawling on her hands and knees to him. One of his friends asked what she said. He said, "She told me to come out from under that bed and fight like a man."

What amazes me is that so many think their problems will go away with marriage, when in reality they intensify. Conflict does not necessarily mean that the marriage is in trouble or doomed to failure. It can be an opportunity for growth and even intimacy. But there is destructive as well as constructive conflict. Let's look at both.

Destructive conflict manifests itself in a passive, aggressive, or passive-aggressive way.

Would you say that you are more like a wolverine, a turtle, or a skunk? Wolverines have sharp teeth and claws. They use sharp words, and they go for the kill. Turtles, on the other hand, are passive. They stick their head in their shell, clam up, may even go away. And then there is the skunk. The skunk is passive, but he can really stink up the place.

Wolverines are more aggressive in nature. We need to constantly pray that God would set a guard over our mouth (Psalm 141:3). We see things and we just want to deal with it. It is the person who "takes no crap," who "puts up with no stuff." They would rather win the argument at the expense of losing the relationship. The poet Ogden Nash says, "If you want your marriage to sizzle with love in the cup, when you are wrong admit it, and when you are right shut up." Name calling, or reaching back into the past with a "remember when you ..." is fighting dirty. Wolverines enjoy mudslinging, and when the fight is over there is mud all over their spouse, the walls and themselves.

Turtles love the silent treatment. They avoid all conflict at all costs. They love to sweep things under the rug, and they like to think it goes away. (It does not, by the way.) Turtles have the idea that, "I won't speak until he apologizes." Or, "I won't respond until she rights this wrong." And what you have is a standoff. No conversation happens. Nothing ever gets resolved. Nothing ever changes. And we leave things out there that give opportunity, at some point, for one or both to reach back in the past with a "Remember when ...."

And then there is the skunk. Skunks avoid direct confrontation, but they speak, all right. They manifest rebellion, stubbornness, and subtle insults. They inwardly seethe and boil, while outwardly saying, "I'm good." Again, nothing gets resolved.

Constructive conflict has some guiding principles.

Be honest. Put away the lying, exaggeration and embellishment, and speak truth in love. Stick to the issue and show respect.

Keep things under control. Use self-control and discipline. Avoid the angry words and name calling. Do not make threats of leaving or divorce. Avoid hurtful and unforgettable words like, "I knew I never should have married you." And avoid all comparisons! Never say, "Why can't you be like …?" or "Why can't you act like …?"

Remember that timing is everything. Do not jump your spouse when they walk through the door. If things get over-heated, back off, wait, and try again later.

Be willing to compromise. No one, especially the same one, should always get his or her way.

Most importantly, keep it private. Never attack or argue in public. Do not go to friends and exaggerate the problem and put them in the middle. Do not run to your family and bash your spouse and then wonder why they still have a problem with your spouse at Thanksgiving dinner.

If you need help, go to a Christian counselor. That will be a safe place for both of you.

Dawn has already told you that we both hate conflict. Therefore, we have always struggled with fighting well. She has also told you that I do not think most things are worth the fight. I know there will be conflict, I am just amazed at what people are willing to go to war over. So many fight over the silliest, most trivial things. Not every hill is worth dying on. Decide between the two of you if it is worth fighting for. If it is, then fight well. And that basically means always attack the problem — and not the person.

DAWN

I really love rollercoasters at theme parks. I just do not like them in life. I like for life to run smoothly on a straight path.

But so often marriage feels more like a rollercoaster. Things are going smoothly, but then you go around a curve and you feel like you hit a wall. You may even be trudging uphill, and that is okay until you get to the top and you go flying down into what seems like a valley. But that is life, and therefore that is so often marriage as well.

Dealing with conflict is never easy, but sometimes it is dealing with what lies within the conflict and beneath our anger that gets us. As Eddie said, being honest and attacking problems together is necessary and can take the sting out of the hurt.

I remember when I was young and how conflict and un-reconciled feelings hurt relationships within my family. Friends, that is never worth it. People and relationships trump stuff every single time. Jesus must have known we would have relationship issues, and He placed a high premium on recon-ciliation. He tells us in Matthew 5:23-24 to leave our gifts at the altar and make reconciliation with our brother first. Jesus placed a higher priority on our relationships being right than He did on our gifts and offerings. A lack of forgiveness, and holding grudges, destroys people and relationships. So often we hold on, thinking that to let go would make what they did to us right. It does not make it right; it makes us right. A lack of forgiveness hurts the person holding onto it more than the person we are at odds with. We do not want that to be true of us in any relationship, but especially in our marriage relation-ship. It is not worth it. It will never be worth it.

Read what John and Noelle say about learning to deal with

conflict when you are used to dealing with it very differently:

John and Noelle: In our culture of individualism, it has become a natural tendency to make self the priority. The culture of individualism undermines the maximal definition of marriage. Northwestern sociologist Eli Finkel observes that we live in a culture in which the needs of self take priority over all other needs. I (John) remember going into marriage carrying all these things I've come to learn in life and expecting Noelle to fall right in line as if she found someone who had all the answers and was ready for me to lead the way. In the same sense, I (Noelle) grew up in a family of what I perceived as strong-willed, self-sustaining women. I remember the first time John met my family while we were dating. After spending an afternoon at my parents' house, he turned to me and said, "Now I see where you get it from!" I had my own ideas and answers and was ready to show John all the "right" ways to do things. This is the definition of selfishness: to believe you have the answers, and anyone in your path is lucky to have your wisdom. In reality, marriage is the joining of two complex and well-formed individuals. We both had twenty-five years of experiences that had formed us into the people standing at the altar as we shared vows.

If marriage has taught us anything, it's that we are a sum of our past experiences and the ways we choose to react to and grow from them. My (John) selfish self was going into the marriage with Ephesians 5:22 reeling through my head, "Wives, submit yourselves to your own husbands as you do to the Lord" (ESV), but was refusing to understand verse 25 calling husbands to love our wives just as Christ loved the church and *gave himself up for her.* Following the example of Jesus looks more like surrendering than it does standing high and mighty. Jesus relinquished his divine privileges, and Philippians 2:7 says "he made himself nothing by taking the very nature of a servant" (NIV). If God can "make himself nothing," then, men, I think we can lay down our prideful view of ourselves to love our wives well.

I often think of when Elijah called Elisha into the life God had for him. The Scriptures tell us that Elisha burned the plowing equipment, so he had nothing to go back to in his past life. He was stepping into a new life and wanted no backup plans. This is the perfect picture of marriage. Marriage is something you hurl yourself into, burning the boats behind you. Mike Mason, in his book *The Mystery of Marriage,* writes, "We must return to an attitude of total abandonment, of throwing all our natural caution and defensiveness to the winds and putting ourselves entirely in the hands of love by an act of will. Instead of falling into love, we may now have to march into it."

Marriage is the intersection of two very different journeys. We can still vividly remember the first time we sat down to talk about why we were having some conflict in our marriage. Instead of hashing out any current issues, our conversation was led into our pasts. We were raised very differently and grew up in families that were on very different sides of the spectrum. Shockingly, we had never thought that maybe current conflict was happening because we had yet to understand not just how, but *why, we* were reacting to each other the way we were. We were struggling to resolve conflicts in our marriage because we didn't realize they were actually rooted in experiences that took place long before we knew each other. We were failing to acknowledge each other's unique conflict style and the ways our past experiences had shaped us as individuals.

I (John) grew up in a family that didn't have a lot of vocally expressed conflict. When I got mad or upset, I would simply get quiet and decide to play it out and conclude the argument inside my head. I had already worked it out within myself and came out the other end fine, but this excluded Noelle from understanding how I had come to my conclusions. While it's great to process the argument and work it out, the process of how you came to the conclusion is often more important than the conclusion itself. In healthy conflict, it's usually the working it out together that grows you closer and stronger. While my family, growing up, wasn't filled with a ton of conflict, my inclination was to forgive quickly so there wasn't any anger. This just led to suppressed feelings, which isn't healthy. This was not advertised as a way of handling conflict in our household, but I found that I could often "get over it" and cause less waves. I had always associated conflict with vocal anger so I would disassociate with conflict at all cost. When I entered marriage, I brought this same conclusion with me. So when Noelle would vocalize her frustrations with me, I would crawl into a hole and think she hated me, most likely getting ready to divorce me the next day.

In contrast, I (Noelle) grew up in a household that vocalized what we were feeling when we were upset, sometimes to a fault. From my perspective, it was better to "get it all out" and possibly have to apologize later, than to sweep our conflicts under the rug. Research has shown that when a married couple argues, the woman actually sees it as a growing experience, that it actually builds a closer bond. On the contrary, men's heart rates skyrocket to a state comparable to that of a man in warfare during a heated argument. I specifically remember an argument where I was openly expressing my opinions and feelings and felt as if I was getting nothing back from John. I remember saying, "Yell at me! Act like this matters to you. Act like you care at all about what I'm saying!" Because of my past experiences with family as well as past relationships, I had associated yelling with passion. I was yelling because I cared. However, I failed to realize that John was silent because he cared, too. What I saw as a healthy experience to create a stronger bond made John think our marriage was crumbling.

We are largely summations of our upbringings and shaped by the many years of life we've lived before we stand next to each other, sharing vows and merging our two life journeys into one. After sitting down and explaining to each other why we do the things we do and how we were shaped by our families and past relationships, we could then begin to better understand each other and discuss how to experience healthier conflict. We also have realized that just because that's how we were raised, it doesn't mean it is right. And when you realize your way is not always the best way, you tend to be much more humble. Choosing to continually learn the terrain of each other's past journeys in order to step into something new has been the best thing for our marriage. Although it is a lifelong process, we are now beginning to use our past as a catalyst for growth rather than an excuse for maladaptive behavior. Rather than one person having all the answers, we are now forming our own path to navigate together, hand in hand.

EDDIE

The definition of friendly fire is weapon fire coming from one's own side, especially fire that causes accidental injury or death to one's own forces.

How terrible that is when we are referring to our military and first responders. But it is equally terrible when that happens within the walls of our home. We need to be good at conflict resolution. We need to learn how to work together as a team and fight for the good of the marriage and the family, not constantly firing at one another. Dawn and I come from different backgrounds, and our families dealt with things differently, so we have had to work hard at figuring out this particular area. Communication never seems to be a problem until there is a disagreement. Successful couples solve problems well; they forgive well, and they forget well. It is laughable to think that there will never be conflict, that we will always agree with one another. Frustrations lead to conflict. Expectations give rise to conflict. They arise from small irritations, like where to squeeze the toothpaste, or whether the toilet paper rolls from over the top or underneath. There are major issues, from how to handle finances to how to raise children. It comes down to letting go of our selfishness and choosing forgiveness. Giving up our will for another is never easy, but it will be required of us if we are going to have healthy marriages.

Isaiah 55:6 says, "Seek the Lord while he may be found; call on him while he is near" (NIV).

That is what we need to do together throughout marriage — but especially in times of conflict, when we need to be working together and not pulling apart.

Hebrews 12:14 encourages us, even commands us, to pursue peace and holiness. Pursuing holiness makes us more like Jesus, and partakers of the divine nature. We want to be effective and fruitful, so we pursue Christlike character, and we turn from sin because sin will never deliver on its promises. It causes us to be enslaved and at war with God and each other. There is no better way to glorify God in our daily lives than to have peaceful and unified marriages. Our marriages are a picture of the gospel. They have the power to draw others to Jesus or turn them away. As Christ has loved us and forgiven us to the point of laying down His life for us, may we do that for one another. That is our calling: daily loving and forgiving one another, laying down our agendas, our preferences, our toys, our plans, our dreams, for one another.

"All men make mistakes, but married men find out about them sooner." — *Red Skelton*

Chapter Three

SOS

"The problem is not the problem. The problem is your attitude about the problem." — Jack Sparrow, Pirates of the Caribbean

EDDIE

In 1928 a mechanic was working on his Ford automobile. He tried all he knew but could not get his car started. So, dejected and disgusted, he sat on the hood and contemplated how he could get rid of the piece of junk. A few minutes later a shiny new Ford pulled up, and a distinguished well-dressed man stepped out and said, "Can I help you?" "Well, I've tried and tried, and I can't fix it." So the man looked under the hood and said, "I see your problem," and immediately fixed it. The owner of the car said, "Thank you, but I did not get your name." "My name is Ford, Henry Ford. I designed the car, so I should know how to make it run."[3]

God designed the family. He ordained marriage. So He knows how to make it run. Maybe it is time we stop relying on our own limited knowledge and wisdom. We need to stop listening to all the other outside voices who call themselves experts, the famous voices we listen to, and listen to the master designer and architect of marriage and family.

Right at the conclusion of the greatest sermon ever preached, the Sermon on the Mount, preached by Jesus, there is the story of two home builders. Jesus tells us the most important part of home-building is not what you build or how you build, but where you build. I think we would all agree it would be better to build a cabin on a firm foundation than a mansion in a swamp.

The true story is told of a builder in Canada who developed a subdivision of very elegant and expensive homes. These were homes valued around a half-million dollars, and that was several years ago. On the outside it was a beautiful subdivision. Time passed, winter came, snow fell, winds blew, and the homeowners began to notice cracks. Then all of a sudden one house collapsed, and then another began to collapse and sink into deep holes. Authorities investigated. He had built the subdivision on a landfill, a garbage dump. He had taken shortcuts in preparing the site, and the results were devastating.

Jesus tells the story of two men who built homes; one home stood the storm, the other did not. The difference was not in the men who built the homes and their skill levels, nor was it in the materials used to build the home. The difference was in the foundation. Jesus said one man was wise and the other one was foolish. The storm just revealed which one was which.

You see, both houses experienced the storm. The winds blew, the rain fell, and the floods came to both homes. Yet one falls and the other stands.

You can walk through any neighborhood, and the homes may look similar. But no matter how they look from the outside, the insides of homes are very different. Some have families that are barely surviving, while others are thriving. One house has a couple whose marriage will last "till death do us part," and another house has a couple who will not last until the next week.

What is Jesus telling us? Simply this: Every single home faces problems and pressures. Every home faces sickness, stress, loss. The rain represents the pressure from above, the flood is the pressure from beneath, and the wind is the pressure from all around.

Whether your home is a Christian home or not, storms will come. Spouses will not always get along. Children will rebel. Jobs will be lost. Finances will create stress. Sickness will visit. Sexual needs and differences will cause arguments. Other factors such as drugs and alcohol may play a role. Pornography may cause hurt and feelings of betrayal. How we deal with those things will cause us to pull together, or it will pull us apart.

DAWN

When Eddie and I got married, I was a young nineteen-year-old, mature in many ways for my age, which maybe is not saying much, but up to my eyeballs with insecurities. I came with baggage that I was not even aware of until the "I will" had been said and we were well into marriage. God used marriage to press His finger on so many of my issues. The ones I was aware of, I thought marriage would solve. The ones I was unaware of would come spilling out in ways that made me wonder who in the world I was. I had no idea who I was. I tried to suppress the insecurity by controlling everything and everyone, including Eddie. I tried to suppress emotions that I knew were unhealthy and that I had become fairly capable at hiding. You know — just keep the monster down. The problem with suppressing things is that at some point they will bubble to the surface. My idea was, like so many other young marrieds, maybe older marrieds too, I thought as long as we both love Jesus and love each other, everything will be fine. The problem is I went to Jesus for salvation when I was younger, but I went to Eddie for my joy and happiness. And Jesus would put me through the wringer and even take me to the woodshed more than a few times to prove to me that Eddie was not responsible for my happiness. I had no clue at that time that marriage was not about my happiness; it was about my holiness. So when I was not happy, it was his fault. Or so I thought. I promise you, if you will stop looking to your spouse to make you happy, you will be happier. And they will be happier too. No one should have to live up to that. No one can survive under that weight. We were not created to do that. The hard lesson I had to learn is that Jesus will never allow another person to fill the void that He has set aside for Himself to fill in our lives. *Never*!

EDDIE

What we have in marriage is two imperfect, selfish people with issues. Each brings their baggage into a relationship where the two are to become one. We are to live in harmony. Maybe that is why marriage is hard. Did anyone ever tell you it would be hard?

I did premarital counseling with a couple one time and asked them some basic questions. Do you have a job? No. Do you have insurance? No. Do you have any money in the bank? No. Do you have a place to live? No. You think you are going to make it? Of course, we love each other!

No one ever succeeds at anything without great effort. A survey was taken of successful people trying to find the common ingredient that led to success. The results were interesting. Some were introverts. Some were extroverts. Some were brilliant, some had average or below-average intelligence. Some had PhDs, while others had little or no education. The one common ingredient for all was that they had a desire to be successful. They were committed to the task. These successful people had problems and struggles, but they had the desire and determination to work through them. We have to have that determination in marriage. Marriage is not easy. We cannot go into marriage thinking it is easy, and we cannot go into marriage with the mindset that, "Well, if it doesn't work out, we can always get a divorce." Every single marriage has problems, to one extent or another. I believe our problems are magnified in the home because that is where we let our hair down, and our feelings and emotions come out. We vent our frustrations on those we love the most.

DAWN

We lived in one of our homes for seventeen years. When we moved into that home our children were ages three, four, six, and nine. That house went through four children who grew into four teenagers, two dogs, and two adults. We did not just live in that house, we LIVED in that house, if you get my drift. We had a pool and a yard that lent itself to be the place for birthday parties, cookouts, barbecues, sleepovers, and all sorts of family and friend life. We wanted it to be the place where our kids wanted to bring their friends rather than go out all the time. We wanted them at home, and we wanted their friends to consider it a home away from home. When we moved, the house was well worn. There were stains in the carpet, smudges on the walls, doors that needed to be fixed, all kinds of things. Not to mention the number of things we had saved and stored in the attic because we did not have the heart (or I did not have the heart) to get rid of them. Boxes of every math sheet, every poem from first grade on. You get it. It was a job getting that house in order and ready to sell. I did not regret the living we had done, I just regretted not having made adjustments or corrections along the way.

How often in life do we fail to make adjustments along the way? We know things are not quite right, but we ignore it. How often do we suppress an emotion rather than sitting down and having a conversation about it? I was, maybe still am, the queen of that. I just want peace. What I have had to learn is that we can say peace all day long, but if we are not honest with each other, there really is no peace.

Or, maybe for you, you do not suppress, you explode. And when it is over, you feel so much better, but you have left untold damage with your words and accusations.

Perhaps your thing is vengeance. Your motto is, "I will not get mad, I will get even." And so you take action that destroys trust and creates bitterness and resentment.

We all have our ways of dealing with our stuff. Unfortunately, when it comes to repairing the damage, we do the bare minimum. Instead of saying, "I'm sorry," we just sweep it under the rug and hope time heals. Or maybe we manage to mumble, "I'm sorry," but we never sit down and talk through where all that emotion came from. I learned recently from a young wife who was describing an argument with her husband about cold fries, but it really was not about the fries. Honestly, it is almost never about the fries. There is always a deeper issue. Usually, it can be tied to whether we feel heard, understood, and supported.

It is a lot like health. We want to feel better. We want to look better. We just do not want to do what it is going to take to get there. We do not want to eat better because of our love affair with sugar and caffeine. We do not want to take vitamins because we do not want to spend the money. We do not want to go to the gym or work out because that would mean getting off the couch and moving. We just want a quick fix, and there is no quick fix for your health, just like there is no quick fix for your marriage.

EDDIE

We have already mentioned some of the problems and points of conflict in marriage, but I do not believe any of those are the biggest problems. I believe that the biggest problem in every marriage is selfish independence. Read Isaiah 53:6. We have all gone our own way.

It makes sense, because in our world today it is all about me. We are told to look out for number one. I deserve a break today. What is in it for me? What can you do for me today? It permeates our society and our marriage relationships.

When we are young, we are dependent on others to take care of us. Then we become independent. We make our own decisions. We become self-sufficient and take care of ourselves. The problem is we reach this stage and we want to stay there. We are to enter the stage of interdependence, where we depend on one another. You take care of the needs of others as well as your own. We take and assume responsibility. The problem comes in marriage when our attitude is, "I'm going to do my own thing and look after myself and my needs."

Now you put together a husband and wife, add two or three kids, and everyone is living in the independent stage. You are in for problems. You have four or five different opinions, and every family member is seeking to live for number one. You are on shaky ground. Do not just shrug and say, no big deal, it will work itself out. It will not.

I can talk to men all day and ask them, what do you want in marriage? They will immediately start talking about what they want their wife to do for them. I want a wife who takes care of the children, keeps the house clean and picked up, is waiting at the door when I get home to greet me with a kiss, have my supper ready and on the table, is great in bed, and who is always telling me how smart and wonderful I am. Sounds good, doesn't it, men?

I can also talk to women and ask them what they want in marriage. They will immediately start talking about what they want their husbands to do for them. I want a man who comes home from work and says, as he hands me roses and candy, "I couldn't wait to get home and be with you. What can I do for you honey? Let me wash those dishes. Don't cook, I'm taking you out. Do not worry about cleaning this house — I am hiring a cleaning company to do that for you. And while I am at it, I am going to hire you some help with these kids." You could live with that, right, ladies? That is what we want, because we are so consumed with self.

When I was praying about marrying Dawn, I kept asking God if she was the one for me. Translated: Is she going to be the one who meets my needs, who makes me better, completes me? I had to change my prayer to: Am I the one for her? Am I the one who will be able to meet her needs, who will make her better?

Husbands, if we knew all Scripture the way we know "Wives, submit to your husbands," we would be biblical scholars and the spiritual leaders in our home that we should be. We are to love our wives as Christ loved the church. There was no selfish independence when He died for the church.

So with all of this said, how do we have a solid foundation

for our homes?

One way is we have active communication. We will talk more in detail about communication in another chapter, so let's just say that communication is key. And communication is not all about talking; it is also about listening. And listening involves hearing and asking questions, making sure we are on the same page.

A solid foundation also comes from moral consistency. Jesus talked about the man who heard the words of Jesus but did not put them into action. It is not enough to read the Bible; we have to do what it says. It is not enough to know what is right; we have to do what is right.

There also needs to be spiritual commitment. Psalm 127:1 says that unless the Lord builds the house, those who build labor in vain. The difference between the two home builders may seem minor, but it is really major. Only one did what God said. Only one of them did what was right. The solid foundation must be Jesus. He is the rock on which we must build our homes. The real foundation of a home is not material or financial. It is spiritual. The storms will come, and without the spiritual foundation, the house will fall.

What this does not mean is that as long as we are Christians, everything should be fine. Christian families divorce as much as non-Christian families. What is the difference? Are we Spirit-controlled, Spirit-led believers seeking to live for Jesus, or are we Christians in name only — saved, but living our own way?

DAWN

The problem is not that problems will come. The problem is we ignore them. The alarm sounds when something is wrong — something is out of sync, we are on different pages — but instead of dealing with it, we hit the snooze button. We ignore the warning signs. Every single time there is a shooting, the question is always asked, "Were there any warning signs?" There are always warning signs. We may not see them. We may be too busy to deal with them. We may be too apathetic to care. But there are always warning signs. Eddie and I have been through things before that have left me thinking, how did we get here? How did we go on like this for so long?

In 2 Chronicles 36, we see that as soon as problems were perceived, the warnings would go off. Alarms are sounding. Are we oblivious? Are we too busy? Are we too focused on others and their lives? What if we checked the warning lights and dealt with issues before we had to suffer the consequences?

We lived in a city years ago when a hurricane blew through. We were warned that it could hit our city hard, but we ignored the warnings. We relied on our own logic. We thought we were too far inland for it to be bad. I remember in the wee hours of the morning, Eddie telling me we needed to wake up Chrissie, our only child at the time, who was two, and get into the hall. The storm was getting worse, and there were tornado warnings. The only thing I heard him say at that moment was, "We need to wake up Chrissie." Our two-year-old. Hmm. Was it really that bad? Because things were getting ready to be much worse if we woke her up. And then I got angry. Did he not tell me there was no need to leave town and go up state to my parents' house? Did he not tell me there was no need to buy water and fill up our bathtubs? Did he not tell me that we did not need to buy batteries for the radio? And now, he is telling me to wake up our two-year-old and keep her in the hallway with me while he sits in the car in the garage to listen to the radio? I remember thinking I would hate to die mad at him, so I decided to table the anger. Instead, I spent the next hours fighting with my two-year-old to keep her safe, and praying because it is the one time in my life I remember thinking we were definitely going to die. You could feel the pressure on the house as it shook. I kept waiting for the roof to blow off. We could hear our tall pines landing on our house as they snapped and fell. The next morning the sun was out and the sky was blue, but our house and yard looked like a war zone. We did not heed the warnings and were totally caught off guard. And we lived through what felt like a war.

I had a friend years ago who had an affair. It is like we could all see it coming, but we could not stop it. Like a train wreck. Things were tense at home. There were problems, but they failed to heed the warning signs. They hit the snooze button when the alarm was sounding. I remember asking her one day, "Was there no time when you were headed to meet this other man that something in you did not scream, 'Stop the car, turn around, end this?'" When we tune out those warnings, we find ourselves in some deep pits.

How much better off we would be if we stopped focusing

on others and focused on ourselves. Not in a selfish way. I just mean, stop thinking, "I wish we were like them," or, "I wish we had that," or whatever. What if we just took fifteen minutes every day to sit down and talk about the emotions of the day with our spouse? What if we focused more on what is good and right with our spouse and our marriage than on what is wrong? Social media is killing us; we look at others' lives and think it is always picture-perfect for everyone else. Every day is not a goosebumps day. Every day is not an Instagram post-perfect day. Just like with porn, it is fantasy. So often what is put out there is what people want others to think of them, not the reality of how things truly are. We all need to stop the comparison. Stop thinking her husband is better than yours and her kids act better than yours. We have to rewire how we think. We have to be transformed by the renewing of our minds, as Romans 12:2 tells us.

I don't know what the ongoing point of conflict is for you. Maybe it is money, time, sex, exhaustion, children, communication, lack of affection or respect, a lack of friendship or lack of trust. But I do know how easy it is for resentment to set in, especially post-children, when you are both exhausted and burning the candle at both ends. I also know how the Enemy is always lurking, looking for an opportune moment to pounce. I know how it is to be angry at your spouse over petty things, and sometimes you do not even know why. So often it is little things that have built up over time, and sometimes it is big things that are choking the life out of us. Sometimes trust has been breached and there is a lot of work to be done. When that is true, get help. If you could fix things, you probably already would have. There is no shame in getting help. Go back, even if it is years in the past; go back to the point of pain, and get to work.

John Gottman, in his research, says that in seventy percent of miserable marriages, someone did something to change the misery. They either left the marriage, or they sought counsel. Thirty percent stayed in the misery and did nothing. Most of the thirty percent stayed due to religious reasons. They wanted to uphold the covenant of marriage. The problem is there was no concern for how they were treating each other.[4] Nothing changes if we do nothing. Choose to change the only person you can: yourself.

EDDIE

So let's just get real, even raw, and talk about the hard places, the slippery slopes. These slippery slopes can be places that can be used to grow us and change us, places where God can receive glory and we can use our experiences to help others. Or they can become hard places. Places where we refuse to change because that is "just how I am." Places we justify and excuse ourselves into thinking we are not to blame, and we maintain the attitude, "It is what it is."

One slippery slope that can lead to a hard place is our finances. Finances make everyone's top five list of hard places; for some it is number one. According to Dave Ramsey, in most marriages, one spouse is a saver and one is a spender. And that will cause conflict every time. How do we spend our money? How much do we spend? How much do we give? How do we prioritize spending our money? She wants this. He needs that. It is no longer "till death do us part" but instead has become "till debt do us part." Debt is easy to slip into because credit is so easy to get. So we live beyond our means, spend money we do not have to acquire things we do not need, to impress people we do not even know or like, and we believe that one day we will be able to pay it off. However, interest on the debt grows, and we get deeper and deeper and deeper.

We choose to suppress instead of talking with our spouse to avoid the ugly argument. We do not have time to take a financial course that would help us, or sit down with an advisor. And on and on it goes.

We have got to want it in order to work at it and get out of this hard place of financial burden, which is wreaking havoc on our marriages. There is no quick fix. It took a while to get there, and it will take a while to get out.

Let me give you a good starting place. Acknowledge and own the fact that God owns everything. It is not my money, my house, my cars, my vacation home. (By the way, if you are in debt, you need to sell the vacation home.) It all belongs to God, and we are stewards. What kind of steward are you? What kind of steward am I with what God has given me? We came into this world with nothing, we will leave with nothing, and what we have in the meantime is on loan from God.

So, if everything belongs to God, then every financial decision we make must glorify Him. The late Christian financial counselor, Larry Burkett, used to say that every financial decision is a spiritual decision.

DAWN

When we say that the two will become one, that includes our finances. We should both be involved in financial decisions. Secrets on spending are always a bad idea.

We have had friends who have things they order sent to the office so their spouse will not find out. In case you are wondering, that is not okay. It is not okay to have private accounts or money stashed away … "just in case."

We have also always told young couples that both need to be involved in decisions about budgeting and how money is spent, but the one who is more gifted in the area should be the one who manages it. I used to manage our accounts, but Eddie took over when we both realized I did not care where every single penny went, and he did. Therefore, he became the one who paid the bills and kept up with everything. It does not automatically need to be the husband's responsibility. Our sons' wives are both extremely gifted in this area, so we encourage them to take the lead in it. It does not make the man less of a man. Remember, we are a team, and we are working together for the good of all things in our marriage.

Eddie and I both love to give. Whether it is a need with our family or strangers, we love having the means to give toward it. The most discouraging times we had financially were when we were strapped and could not do that. Eddie has more of the gift of giving, so it was always more difficult for him when we did not have extra to give to others. One of our married children even goes so far as to have it set aside in their budget — not only their tithe, but an amount they can give to others during the month. That is a great way to be intentional and not end up at the end of every month wondering where it went, or being disappointed that there is nothing left over to share. We always want to have some leftovers to share, or something set aside in case God asks us to do something out of the ordinary. We never want finances to be so tight that we have to say no when God says go.

EDDIE

Sickness can be another slippery slope that leads to a hard place. My dad was sick for most of my life. He actually taught me more in his sickness than he might have in good health. It just depends on our perspective, and allowing it to work for us and not against us.

Our vows say, "In sickness and in health," but let's be real. How many of us give much thought to sickness outside of a cold or headache? Marriage can be tough enough when everyone is healthy, but add in some sickness, whether minor or severe, and we can find ourselves in a hard place.

This was lived out in front of me as my mother cared for my dad for eighteen years. As long as I can remember, he was sick. My dad had the Whipple procedure when I was very young. The Whipple procedure is an operation to remove the head of the pancreas, the first part of the small intestine, the gallbladder and the bile duct. The remaining organs are reat-

73

tached to allow you to digest food normally after surgery. Maybe things are better now for people who undergo that procedure, but in that day it left my dad with a very diminished quality of life. He also developed pneumonia and was prescribed heavy antibiotics, which caused him to lose all his hearing. I am fairly certain that when my mom and dad said, "I do," and vowed to love "in sickness and in health," "till death do us part," they never imagined what that would look like. How could they? But it does mean we do not take our vows lightly. Those words we say, words that we promise, are very real, and God takes them very seriously. As should we.

DAWN

My story is a little different from Eddie's in that sickness came along for my parents later in life.

My mom developed Alzheimer's in her early seventies. If you know anything about that disease, you know how debilitating it is. It is a slow, agonizing, hard-to-watch disease. As my dad would say, "To see someone who at one time was so active and vital slowly waste away — not only forgetting people she has known her entire life, but forgetting how to eat, how to do the very simple things of life, even to the point of death, when they forget how to take a breath — is heartwrenching." I watched my dad care for her, refusing to allow any other kind of care until her final three weeks of life, when hospice entered the scene. He would tell me how people would offer to sit with her so he could go out some and enjoy himself. He told me time and again that he did not want to go out; he wanted to be right there at home with her. I would go once a week to sit with her so he could go to the grocery store or get his hair cut. I would always tell him to take his time, but he never did. He just wanted to be back home with her. And trust me: Caring for someone with Alzheimer's is extremely difficult. It was not just sitting with her. It was exhausting. At times she would become belligerent and aggressive. She would fall and he would have to pick her up. And it was twenty-four hours a day, seven days a week.

My dad was a heart patient and diabetic. His last ten years were difficult, caring for my mom, but he was doing very well with his health and controlled his diabetes with diet. But I remember how hard it had been on my mom when he had his heart attack years earlier. I remember her staying by his side, not wanting to leave the hospital. They were both lost without the other one.

Those are the sicknesses we don't plan on. We somehow think we will escape the "big" sicknesses and that our children will stay healthy; yet we do not, and they do not.

We have friends who have small children with cancer. We have friends where one or both spouses have serious diseases. We have friends, young and old, who know what it is like to battle sickness and disease every day.

One of the pieces of advice I gave all four of our children before they married was, "Make sure you love them — a lot." Because I could point to my parents or remind them of my in-laws and tell them, "So often, this is what it looks like." If you marry because you are "in lust" or are trying to escape something, or you just think there will not be another opportunity to get married, or you are getting older, or lonely, or whatever else, you will have a difficult time if some of these realities hit.

Eddie and I are both strong believers in health and wellness. You only get one temple, and we believe God expects us to take care of it. We are gym rats four days a week; we walk, we run, we lift weights, we try to eat a healthy diet, we take a lot of supplements. We have cleaned a lot of toxic chemicals out of our house, and we choose essential oils over other types of remedies. We even take targeted supplements for things such as Alzheimer's and heart disease, because we believe that we can reverse the pattern with good choices. But we also know that all that does not necessarily guarantee us health. Some things, we cannot control. However, that does not excuse us from doing all that we can to live a healthy lifestyle.

EDDIE

What about the slippery slope of drugs and alcohol? Those can certainly lead to a hard place. The entire subject of drink/ do not drink can be debated for all time. But I do not think there is much debate when we speak of substance abuse. We know firsthand the problems of drug abuse. We have seen way too many lives ruined, and families shattered (not to mention health destroyed), with addiction and abuse. For those who grew up in an atmosphere of abuse, you know the negative effect it has. My father was a heavy drinker most of his life. I really was unaware until I was in high school. It was never very evident because he was a mellow abuser instead of a violent abuser, but it contributed to his health problems, and he died from cirrhosis of the liver. Some would say that it created a violent, angry atmosphere in their home. Some would say there was constant conflict due to abuse. Prescription drug abuse can cause many of the same problems in a home. Anything that causes change in personality and creates fear and abuse of any kind is a slippery slope that leads to hard places.

DAWN

One of the things we had to talk to our children about was the fact that alcohol abuse ran in our family, on Eddie's side. We wanted them to be aware that genetics can play a role and could cause them to have a tendency toward addictive behaviors if they chose to drink. We cannot make a biblical argument for a teetotal lifestyle. We can only tell you that addiction and abuse can cause untold heartache and problems. For those with more addictive personalities — and yes, some prove that with phones, technology, all sorts of things — there just needs to be some care and accountability taken.

EDDIE

Pornography. It is nothing to play with. It is as addictive as any drug out there, and it causes so much harm. Feelings of betrayal and hurt linger long after apologies have been made, and trust is something that will be lost and will have to be regained through hard work. Porn is easy-access. One click of the finger and it is in front of you. The tendency is to believe you are not hurting anyone and it is no big deal. It is a very big deal. Intimacy with your spouse suffers. Real intimacy is when we totally love and give ourselves to our spouse. Porn is when we give ourselves to something else. It involves hiding and withholding a part of ourselves from our spouse. It also replaces a real relationship with imitation. There is a focus on the physical, where the physical is enhanced to look more attractive.

In the 1950s, a Dutch biologist named Nikolaas Tinbergen discovered which markings and color patterns on female butterflies were the most attractive and alluring to male butterflies. He made cardboard female dummy butterflies with those attractive markings, and the male butterflies were more attracted to the dummy butterflies, even trying to mate with them.[5] Porn is no more real than dummy butterflies.

DAWN

The real purpose of sex is destroyed and twisted when porn is part of the equation. Sex is a wonderful gift given by God, intended for married couples. Porn twists and perverts that. It is self-absorbing and selfishly oriented. It is something you do for yourself in order to please yourself. God-honoring married sex is about giving love and affection. Porn is all about me and my satisfaction at the expense of my spouse. Great sex happens when we focus on pleasing our spouse and not on getting our own needs met. From what I hear, read and observe, porn may be right there with finances — more so than drugs and alcohol — as the hardest place and slipperiest slope in marriage today. And do not think that this is a man-only problem. Studies tell us that more and more women are becoming addicted to pornography. It now starts at a very young age and it is causing even young married couples sexual problems that they should not be facing. It is a destroyer of love and intimacy.

EDDIE

Work — or perhaps we should say workaholism — is rarely thought about in terms of causing a hard place in marriage, but like everything else, when abused, it breeds hurt. Years ago, before heading into ministry, I received some solid advice from several pastors. I asked them, if you could give me one piece of advice concerning ministry, what would it be? Without hesitation, they all said, "Put your family first. I neglected mine, and it cost me." One told me that the church was his mistress and his wife greatly resented it. He could not stop crying. The other said the church was his wife; he was married to the church and that was wrong. He said, "The church is the bride of Christ."

I will be honest with you. Church people will turn on you. I did not get that in my early days of ministry, but I get it now. I have poured time and effort and energy into people, and they have turned on me. Same with staff. I have given some staff members opportunities when people said they didn't deserve it; given second, third — more chances when people warned me about them — and they turned on me. Leaders have turned. Members have left for another church. And it hurts. But your family will be there through all of it if you do not neglect them and you love them well.

I know how hard it is for those of us with a strong work ethic, and especially those who do not work nine-to-five jobs. For some of us, our work is never done. We have to learn to leave it. I have not always done that well. There were times my wife would tell me, "Your body is here, but you are not here." Learning balance, how to have margin, is a skill we must learn. We will last longer. I know some who look down the road, and they want to retire early, so they feel like they have to pay on the front end, but that is usually when we have young families and they need us the most. Those early years are precious, and we will not get them back.

Some say they just love what they do. That is great. Just love your family more.

My plan is to pastor until I am seventy. I realize I need margin and have to pace myself and take care of myself to avoid burnout.

There are always seasons where it is busier and we may have to work harder and longer during those times, but it comes down to priorities.

Are you a workaholic?

When you relax, do you feel guilty?

We all need a sabbath. We need times of rest and relaxation.

Burnout is a real thing. It can be a slippery slope that leads to a hard place.

DAWN

Life always seemed the most crazy after we would make a move. Thankfully, I was a stay-at-home mom, so I could try and get some normalcy to our home life fairly quickly, but it was always an adjustment. It was always hardest on Eddie, as he would work long hours trying to learn a new system, pray for vision, and then work to carry it out in a place that was used to doing things a particular way. They were trying to get used to him and he was trying to get used to them, and it just took a lot out of him on the front end. I remember moving to a new place in early June right after school was out. I loved that, because we had the summer to adjust and get our bearings before school started back. But from early June to early October, we rarely saw Eddie. He would leave about seven in the morning, come home for dinner, and then head back for meetings. He would usually arrive back home well after the kids were in bed. I remember telling him, in one of those "I've had enough, I can't take it anymore" moments, that when he chose to leave and move again, the only ones getting in the car with him would be the five of us. I told him, "No church member or leader here is going to follow you from this place." In other words, "The six of us are what truly matter, and we need more of you and we need to be priority with you." I think from that time things shifted. No, he was not always there for everything. He did not work nine to five with an hour for lunch. But he did begin to prioritize. He learned to say no to things so that when he said yes to something else it meant more. He began to realize that being respected and loved by his kids was a greater win than what others thought of him. And he learned that his wife could handle the home front herself pretty well, but it was a lot better atmosphere in the house when she felt loved by him and connected to him. Everyone's job is different. It has different demands on time, travel, stress, whatever. But balancing things for a home that reflects an attitude of gratefulness for the family God has blessed us with is worth the extra work and tender loving care.

Even being empty nesters, we still have to find balance with work. Eddie's job is still never done, and he has to be intentional about leaving things at the office. I work from my phone and absolutely love what I do. But working from my phone also means that work can happen every day, weekends, late at night, even while on vacation. Balance is necessary even when — or maybe especially when — we love what we do.

EDDIE

One of the greatest lessons we can learn is that we are all wired differently, and not everyone in the house thinks and responds like me. Everyone does not like what I like. We are raised differently. We come to marriage with different expectations. We go about things differently. Know each other's story, and the puzzle pieces may make more sense.

Here is Stephen and Kaylin's story: "How Our Differences Make Us Better."

Kaylin: Before we got married, I saw a lot of our similarities. We both loved the Lord, we played sports, we loved the outdoors, and we both enjoyed fitness. It wasn't until after we got married that I saw more of our differences. At first it was frustrating. Stephen didn't move as fast as I wanted him to, and he didn't see the things around the house that needed to be done like I did. Stephen was more of a peacemaker and processed things slower than I did. This made handling conflict interesting. Over time, the Lord revealed to me that He brought us together for a reason and that we benefit from our differences. I'm glad that Stephen is slower to speak than I am and that he likes keeping the peace. It helps me learn how to grow in areas that I struggle with.

Stephen: I thought the best way to find a spouse was to find someone just like me. Because someone just like me is easier to love and to live with. I was looking for myself. Someone who resembled me, who liked the things I liked, who agreed with me and saw things the way I saw things. As a natural introvert, people who are different from me take more energy to be around. Before Kaylin and I got married, there were many personality differences, but we agreed on the essentials. We had similar passions, desires, callings, and a love for Jesus. However, once you get married, it becomes so easy to look at the differences that we may forget the ways we are alike. Early on in our marriage, this created some conflict. How we communicated, how we responded in certain situations, how we received and expressed love were all open season for conflict. Our differences became enlarged. It makes sense why marriage can be a challenge, especially during the newlywed stage. What we were able to eventually do was to identify those differences and find ways to celebrate them rather than allow them to pull us further apart. We've seen how God can take two very different people and draw them closer together. Seeing this has created such balance for us. I have many shortcomings and weaknesses that are very evident at times, and it is in those times where I rely heavily on Kaylin. She always seems to counteract my weaknesses with her strengths. It takes the word "team" to a whole new level.

Kaylin: For me, a big change was when I realized that Stephen was a gift from the Lord. There were so many reasons why God brought us together, and I wanted to appreciate that more. I began to ask God to help me see Stephen the way He sees Stephen. I would ask God to help me see and appreciate the way Stephen was created. Although our personalities are very different, the Lord has helped me extend more grace and understand that not everyone is the same. Everyone is different and was created in a special and unique way.

Stephen: This has helped us in how we love others as well. Naturally, I tend to overlook obvious needs around me, even with friends and family. Kaylin rarely misses a need. She's always quick to see a need and always quick to act. She's always looking for ways to meet the needs of those around her. I love people and have a heart to meet needs; the unfortunate thing is I don't always see them. It's not that I care less than

Kaylin, I just don't notice them as easily. Therefore, our team-work has enabled us to love people better, to use our marriage as a tool and for the good of others. Kaylin also helps me live in the moment. I can't tell you how many times I have zoned out in the middle of a conversation, thinking about what's going on around me, or what's going to happen next, only to be steered back by a loving tap or whisper reminding me to focus on those in front of me.

Kaylin: Correct. Early on, I assumed Stephen didn't care about the things I cared about, that he was being lazy and expected me to do everything, especially around the house. But I've learned that's not the case. Stephen just needed help seeing what needed to be done. And when he learned of the need, he was more than happy to help!

Stephen: Other ways our differences have benefited us is through careers and ministry. I'm more vision-driven. I tend to dream and spend most of my time with my head in the clouds, dreaming and thinking about the possibilities of what could be. My downfall is my inability to put those dreams into action or create practical steps toward accomplishing my goals and dreams. This is where Kaylin comes in. If I'm spending time thinking about the future, Kaylin is busy making today happen. She is thinking through the details and putting plans into action. This has greatly benefited my career, because once Kaylin catches my vision, she's always there to help me bring those plans to life.

EDDIE

I want to share a practical exercise for you to try. It will take some effort, but I believe it will work. The question is, is your marriage and home worth thirty minutes a day for seven days? If so, try this:

Find a place where the two of you can be alone. Have two chairs facing each other and a big alarm clock that ticks. Divide the thirty minutes into six segments.

The first five minutes, think about what it would be like to live life alone. You may remarry, but odds say the second and third marriages have even less a chance of surviving.

The second five minutes, think about your part in the problem. What have you done? We spend all our time focusing on our mate's fault. What is your responsibility in this? Think, do not talk. Some say, "I am not at fault," and that may be your problem. We see the speck in our mate's eye and ignore the beam in our own.

The third five minutes, think about the children and how it will affect them. It will — and perhaps even their children.

The fourth five minutes, begin to talk. Open the Bible and read 1 Corinthians 13.

The fifth segment, talk about the good times you had. It may have been a while ago, but there were good times.

The sixth segment, lean forward, hold hands and pray. You may never have prayed before or together, but pray for God's guidance. Turn it over to Jesus.

If your marriage needs healing, maybe it needs to be totally revived. If it needs a miracle, Jesus is still in the miracle business.

"Marriage is like a deck of cards. In the beginning all you need is two hearts and a diamond. By the end you wish you had a club and a spade."— Author unknown

Chapter Four

Let's talk about it.

"Sometimes I'll start a sentence and I don't even know where it's going. I just hope I find it along the way." — The Office

DAWN

In an era of increasingly fragile marriages, a couple's ability to communicate is the single most important contributor to a stable and satisfying marriage, according to a recent Gallup poll.

What comes to mind when you hear the word communication? For me, and perhaps for many of you, talking comes to mind. We hear so often about the need to communicate clearly. We hear people refer to someone as a great communicator. So naturally we think about talking. But communication means so much more. It is deeper than what we say. Many times, it is what we do not say. And too often it involves a lack of hearing. Communication can be physical, emotional or intellectual.

The definition of communication is the imparting or exchanging of information or news. If that alone were enough, most would say that communication is not a problem in their marriage. I would say that, as well. I have imparted much information to my husband through the years. With a large family, there are many times of imparting information — such as schedules, meal plans, who is picking up whom from where and what time. All that is necessary for a family to function, but it cannot end there. If it does, we cannot say that we have great communication skills with our spouse. And that type of communication will never lead to intimacy, although I will also say that without it, it can lead to a lack of intimacy.

Intimate communication says that we feel understood and accepted for who we are. It means that we trust the other person and open up completely to them without fear of betrayal. That sheds a different light on things. How many of us would say that there is no communication problem with our spouse? Do we always feel heard — not just our words, but the feelings and emotions behind our words? Do we always feel understood after a conversation? Do we leave our conversations feeling accepted and free of any fear? Do we share completely and transparently how we feel?

Communication is definitely not just talking. It is not just relaying information. Communication is understanding what is being said or not said. It involves tone of voice. We talk a lot about tone of voice in our house. It is not always what we say, but how we say it, most of the time. Tone speaks volumes, friends.

We can communicate a lot without words too, can't we? I had this down to a science, or maybe an art form, in the early days of marriage. I believed clamming up and saying nothing was the key to conflict resolution. But that is not true. That is the negative way to communicate without words. The positive side of communicating without words is the ability to be together without the need for words. Now, this certainly is not meant for long stretches of time. I am talking about being able to sit on the porch or in front of the fire or to watch the sunset or sunrise, and there be no need for words. The longer you have been married, the more you know what each other is thinking in those moments. But let me add, those are also amazing settings for great communication with words. They set the stage for peace and calm where great conversation can be had and where everyone leaves feeling understood and heard.

Holding hands is one of my favorite things to do with Eddie. It communicates without a word. It is the non-sexual touch that means so much. It communicates safety and protection. It communicates that we are happy to be together. It tells onlookers that we are a couple, teammates, playmates, friends, lovers.

EDDIE

Several years ago, Dawn told me she thought I was losing my hearing. She said I needed to go and see Greg, an ENT doctor in our church. When I got there, Greg said, "I think your problem may be selective hearing. I see that a lot in men your age who have been married as long as you." Well, to my defense, he did the test and found I did have some diminished hearing. But I think he was also right in his first diagnosis, because from time to time I do suffer from selective hearing.

Listening is essential to good communication. Some people see communicating as them telling someone else what to do. Preachers are often called communicators not because they are good at listening, but because they're good at talking. Some of us are good at telling our opinion, but not very good at receiving the opinions of others. There is an old saying, not biblical, but true: God gave us two ears and one mouth, so we should spend twice as much time listening as talking.

Brian Harbour tells the story of Jorge Rodriguez, a Mexican bank robber, who lived around the turn of the century in the early 1900s. He would slip across the border, go into Texas and rob banks, and flee back to Mexico. After one robbery, a Texas Ranger was hot on his trail. He followed him back over to Mexico and caught up with him relaxing and celebrating in a bar. The Ranger pulled out a .45, pointed it at Rodriguez and said, "I know who you are and what you have done. Unless you tell me where you have hidden all the money, I am going to kill you right here and now." Here is the problem: Jorge did not know a word of English, and the Ranger did not know Spanish. A little problem with communication. The bartender, realizing what was happening, spoke up and said, "I know both languages; I'll translate." He translated to Jorge what the Ranger had said. Jorge said to the bartender in Spanish, "Tell the Ranger I want to live. Go to the old well on the north side of town that is abandoned and remove the stones on the side of the well facing north. All the money is there, every cent of it, millions of dollars." With that, the translator turned to the

Texas Ranger and said, in English, "Jorge says he will never tell, he is a very brave man and not afraid to die. Go ahead and shoot!"[6]

The moral to that story is that inadequate communication can be hazardous to your health. That is true in marriage and family relationships, or any relationship, for that matter. Many feel like they live in the Tower of Babel spoken of in Genesis, where God confused the language.

DAWN

Our boys grew up playing baseball. They played basketball and football as well, but when the time came to really focus on a sport later in high school, they both chose baseball, much to their dad's delight, and they played through college. They are very similar in their interests, but very different in personality. Actually, all four of our children have very distinct personalities, and we had to study them and learn them in order to know what motivated them and how to discipline them. But our boys were very close in age, so they played on the same team in high school. Their coach soon learned what we had learned, and that was, you could not treat them the same. One was motivated by positive affirmation and encouragement. The other loved that as well, but he could be highly motivated by a chewing-out like only a coach could do (at least the coach that they played for). He told us one day that he could go to the mound with one of ours and just chew on him, question his manhood, shame him, and walk away knowing he was going to get the next out and get them back in the dugout because he could see the fire in his eyes. Sure enough, he would commence to throwing bullets, and the poor batter had no chance. Do that to our other son, and you just dug your own grave. He would do nothing to your benefit after that kind of chewing, but if you went out there and told him you believed he could get this next guy out and get out of trouble, he would believe it and make it happen.

I will never forget leaving a game and asking the boys if they could ever hear the cheering of the fans or their name being called on the public address. They both said no, they were too tuned into the game. But one did say, "But I can hear Dad when he sighs and groans, so would you please ask him to stop." That only became funny when the playing days were over, but does that not speak volumes about how we communicate and how we receive it?

It is like that with our love language. So often we give love the way we want to receive it, and it means nothing to our spouse. If my love language is gifts, I can spend a fortune buying gifts for my husband and it is wasted if his love language is not gifts. And then it leads to my misunderstanding and feeling unappreciated because he does not receive it the way I think he should. It is because it does not communicate love to him the way he receives love. That is why studying and learning our spouse is so important, and communication is a key way to do that.

EDDIE

Counselors tell us that one of the biggest problems in marriage is the breakdown of communication, which leads to many other issues.

Issues with sex ... do you talk about it? Do you know what pleases your spouse?

Issues with finances ... do you sit down and talk about it? We are told one partner is usually very tight and one is usually more of a spendthrift. Have you sat down together and tried to get on the same page? Do you work on a budget together?

Issues with in-laws ... do you set boundaries?

Why do we not communicate well about these issues that are so important to us? Maybe because it is hard work. It takes effort, time and energy. We have to want it. We must desire it. We have to make concessions and not insist on our own way. Perhaps we feel as though we will not be heard or that our opinion is never valued, so what is the use?

How often do you actively interact with other members of your family? It has been said that the average father spends seven minutes a week in conversation with his children. The study also revealed that a husband and wife spend twenty-seven minutes in conversation a week. Why? It is not urgent to us, not important, not a priority. Electronic devices can be vices. They may not be creations of the devil, but they can be a tool of the devil. We can say that we are just so busy, that we do not have time, but the study also revealed that children watch four to six hours of television a day, and parents watch three to four. Electronics, earphones, computers, social media, and living life at a breakneck pace add up to very little face-to-face time.

It has been said, "With the invention of the two-bathroom home, we have forgotten how to cooperate. With the two-car home, we have forgotten how to associate. And with the two-plus-television home, we have forgotten how to communicate."[7]

It goes back to what Cool Hand Luke once said: "What we have here is a failure to communicate."

Communication is a challenge, but it is crucial. We are all wired differently. Men are from Mars, women are from Venus. One is on the AM dial, the other on FM. The greatest gift we can give our spouse and our children is the gift of listening.

When we listen, we communicate several important messages:

You are important to me.

Your opinion is valuable to me.

I want to know how you feel.

I want to hear what you have to say.

I will keep my mouth closed and my ears open.

The number one complaint I hear from wives concerning their husbands is, "They do not listen." That is why so many affairs begin with conversation. "He listened to me. My husband doesn't."

What exactly does listening look like? Turn off the TV. Do not look at your phone. Do not be so quick with a solution. Sometimes they do not even want a solution; they just want you to listen. But us "fix-it guys" want to just solve the problem, be the hero and move on.

DAWN

As Eddie said, because we are so different, it makes communication even more important. So many wives — yes, me included — complain that our husbands do not "get us," they do not understand us. It is true that maybe sometimes that is because he is not listening or paying attention. But it is also true that sometimes it is because we are not communicating what we need very well. Ladies, we have to own that one. It would be so nice if they could just read our mind. (Well, probably not all the time, right?) But we live as though they know exactly what makes us tick, what we need, where we are coming from. In reality, we have never even opened our mouths to tell them. Sometimes words are unnecessary, but sometimes they are a must. It is not whining and nagging if we go about it in the right way. The wrong way would be those times we explode and storm out of the room fussing about how "he will never get it." And we think the longer we have been married, the less we should have to explain. Oh, if that were only true. Serving our spouse well and being selfless does not mean suffering in silence. I know that, because I grew up in a home where my mother had zero problem expressing herself, which many times was loud and dramatic, so I was always very guarded with my communication. Instead of communicating in a healthy way, I would just internalize everything. That spilled over into our marriage. I would expect Eddie to just know how I was feeling or leave him to figure it out on his own. I was more afraid of an argument ensuing than trusting that we could talk things out and figure it out together. It is probably one of the things I would love to have a do-over with the most. I am still not great at healthy conversation and voicing my needs and wants and opinions, but I have made a lot of progress. It just has not come easily.

I have always said that Eddie has been quick to help around the house and with the children IF I asked him to help. My problem is I did not want to have to ask. I wanted him to be able to look around and see that I could use a little help. That course of action rarely worked. And I did plenty of suffering in silence when all I had to do was ask — *nicely*. It was not that he was rude or selfish or tried to make me feel like a single parent, he was just unaware. There is a difference. I believe most spouses really do want to love one another well, we just do not always know what that looks like. And it does not help if our spouse is not willing to speak up and trust the process of healthy communication. Remember earlier when we talked about love language and loving our spouse the way they receive love and not the way we receive it? That is because it is so easy to love in ways that mean love to us but may be completely foreign to our spouse. Use a date night to talk about what matters to you in your marriage and what you need from one another. It is exhausting to continue doing the same thing and feel like you are getting nowhere. And be specific. Give one another a visual. Tell them what it looks like to you to feel loved and appreciated.

I remember our son-in-law talking about this when he married our daughter. His love language is Words of Affirmation. He spent much time and effort writing her the sweetest notes and leaving them around the house, and before he would leave for work in the morning. He was discouraged because she never seemed to acknowledge them. What he found out was that was not her love language. She appreciated them, but they did not really do much for her. They needed to reverse things. She needed to be the one leaving notes, and he needed to be buying gifts. And if I can add this while we are on the subject: Love languages *do change*! You may disagree, but most wives would agree. I know mine has changed several times. My love language was Time when we got married, but by the time there were four little ones in the house, it quickly changed to Acts of Service. Now, in the season of life we are in, I am back to Time, but Words of Affirmation and Touch are also important. I think it is one reason marriage is fun. We can never stop learning and growing together. The adventure changes with time, but the journey is always fascinating if we embrace it and continue to grow together.

EDDIE

Let's talk about two kinds of communication: verbal and non-verbal.

Verbal is what you would guess: It is what we say. It is the words we use. James 3:5-6 tells us that the tongue is a fire, a dangerous weapon known to start wars, ruin friendships, start revolutions. It has ruined more reputations, wrecked more homes and split more churches than any other weapon. But it can be used for good. Our family lived in Aiken, South Carolina, for seventeen years. That area is known for SRS, the Savannah River Site nuclear plant. The uranium that is used to build bombs for destruction is also used to produce electricity for good. Proverbs 18:21 tells us the power of life and death is in the tongue.

In Proverbs 15 we see some solid guidelines for the words we use when communicating with our spouse.

Verse 1 talks about gentle words. Let's face it, we all get angry. The problem when we are angry with our spouse is that we say hurtful, hateful things. Or maybe we are the type that when we get angry, we clam up, withdraw. What we communicate non-verbally is that we are mad and do not want to talk about it. But even in anger, we can choose to respond with harsh words or gentle words. Harsh words will stir up anger and block communication. Gentle words will smooth and open the lines of communication.

Proverbs 15:2 talks about wise words. Wise words are honest and loving. When we say hateful things, they may be true, but they are not wise. Dishonesty is a barrier to communication and that is unwise, but speaking truth in love is always best. Telling lies causes us to dig a deep pit, because we continue telling more to cover the first. Wise words are honest and truthful, spoken in love.

We find the importance of healing words in verse 4. Healing words are, as some say, soothing, encouraging, kind. Kind words edify, cruel words crush. The phrase "Sticks and stones may break my bones, but words will never hurt me" is a lie. Words do hurt; they cut and they scar. We give Job's friends a hard time for their loser advice, but they say some good things in Job 4:4: "Your words have steadied the one who was stumbling and braced the knees that were buckling" (CSB).

There is a story of a boy growing up in a small town in Tennessee. His mother was not married, so the reproach that fell on her also fell on him. He was bullied at school, with people often saying, "Who's your daddy?" He became a recluse, and when he was about twelve, a new pastor came to the church in the community. The little boy was intrigued by the new pastor, so he started attending church. He would always come in late and slip out early, afraid of being bullied, even in church. One day things happened quickly; he was caught up in the crowd and found himself face to face with the pastor, who said, "Who are you, young fella? Whose boy are you?" He thought, "Oh no, even the pastor." Then the pastor said, "Wait a minute, I know who you are — God is your father; you are a child of God." Then he said, "Young man, you have a great inheritance, go claim it." That encounter literally changed the direction of that boy's life. The little boy's name was Ben Hooper, who went on to become the twice-elected governor of Tennessee. Kind, encouraging, healing words build up.

Lastly, we see corrective words. Even when words are gentle, wise and healing, they sometimes need to be corrective in nature. One of my pet peeves is when a spouse corrects the other in public over things that do not matter. Again, there will be times for correction, but it should be constructive. Can you handle that? That is why athletics and the military are important for life. Both instill discipline. Learning how to give and receive loving correction is essential to life and key to communication in the home.

Non-verbal communication involves time and place. Timing is everything. Ecclesiastes 8:6 says, "For every activity there is a right time and procedure, even though a person's troubles are heavy on him" (CSB). When we are tired and angry, it is probably not the best time to drop a bomb on your spouse. And in public and in front of others is not the place to have a heavy conversation. Schedule some time to sit down and talk. When the kids were at home, we had to be extremely intentional with this. For us, lunches worked better than dinners because, once they were in school, there was no need for a babysitter, and normally we were wrapped up in their activities in the evening. When they were younger, we did hire sitters so that we could go out occasionally, but usually the plan was to have them on an early bedtime schedule so that we had several hours in the evening at home to ourselves. Now that the kids are grown and out of the house, one of our favorite places is our porch with a fireplace. That is a good talking atmosphere and has a way of breaking down defenses and replacing them with relaxation. And we leave the phones inside. Even empty-nesters have to be intentional. It is too easy to just sit and zone out with no one in the house, scroll through our phones, stay glued to the television.

Another important thing, along with time and place, is body language. Pay attention to yours as well as your spouse's. Experts tell us that sixty to ninety percent of all communication consists of body language, eye contact and facial expressions. I do not always look people in the eye when we talk. I am an introvert. When I lean back, cross my legs, fold my arms, that is comfortable to me. I am not hiding anything. But, I have to be cognizant of that. What am I saying to the person I am conversing with? And men, really listen to your wife. Not only to what she is saying, but what she is not saying. Ever hear, "Don't listen to what I say, listen to what I mean?" That confuses us men. What I mean is, obviously something is wrong — her expression, body language, everything says something is wrong. So we ask, "What's wrong?" She says, "I'm fine." So we go on believing or hoping she really is fine. Usually she is not, guys. Pay attention to her. Learn, study and know your wife. Listen more, talk less, end it well and do not end it until you can end it well. Be willing to compromise and make concessions.

Sounds like hard work. Yes, it is. Maybe even sounds like a lot of trouble. Maybe. But it is worth it. At times we blow it. Seek to restore the relationship. Do not get caught up in things that do not matter, but realize what is a big deal to your spouse even if it is not a big deal to you.

It has been said that blood is to the body what communication is to the marriage relationship. Blood flows through the body, flushing out impurities and adding new life. Communicating well with one another adds life to your marriage.

DAWN

We usually tell couples that if something is not going to matter in five years, be willing to let it go. If it will matter to

103

one or both of you, be willing to have the hard conversation. It is the same with our kids. We knew we could not fight them on everything, so we chose the battles we felt like we had to win and we focused on those. You cannot fight about everything and go to the death about everything with your spouse, either. So you have to pick the battles you believe will lead to a healthier relationship.

Secrets and lies are things that can destroy us. They leave room for mistrust and doubt. We have to be willing to be totally transparent with one another even when it is hard. We may not always agree with one another. We may not always understand one another. But we are open and honest, and we respect one another.

Is it not funny how you sometimes spell things when you are talking so the little ones cannot quite understand? Our granddaughter is trying to learn to spell because she hates when we do that. We will spell something, and she will immediately ask what that spells. Do you not feel like sometimes we need to spell things out with our spouse? I mean, make it as simple as possible so they get it?

Not long ago our daughter-in-law asked our son to stop by the store on his way home and get her a mask. In his efforts at the store to choose the right one, he decided to FaceTime her and ask which one. He was in the cosmetics aisle, assuming she wanted a face masque. The problem is, she was not talking about a face masque. She wanted a face mask because she was going to do some painting. I can tell you right now that Eddie would have come home with a Halloween mask if he could have found one.

I remember how harried our Sundays used to be when the children were all young. We were serving in a very large church at the time, and of course after the service it was my job to gather all four children from their respective places and keep them together until we were ready to leave. That really was not the problem. The problem entered when, after gathering all my little chicks, we would stand around and talk or wait for Eddie to be ready to leave. That always gave my children just enough cushion to venture off and start exploring, like there was something new they were not already familiar with. Normally that meant they would get just outside of my ability to see them, knowing I was cornered talking to someone and could not reel them in. That would lead to the second gathering of the morning before we could go home. We always drove two cars to church, still do. We never have gone to church at the same time, hence the need for two cars on Sunday.

I remember one particular Sunday after arriving home, frazzled as usual, and one child was missing. For those who know us well, you can probably guess which one it was. Stephen, our third child and firstborn son, was known for going off and doing his own thing, not just at church, but everywhere. After the usual headcount, Eddie and I looked at each other and said, "Where is Stephen?" I said to Eddie, "I thought you had him. He always wants to ride with you." And Eddie said to me, "I thought you had him." While I continued to boil and spew, "Do I always have to do everything? Can't you at least help get the kids home from church since I got them up this morning, fed them breakfast, got them dressed and in the car, got them to their class and then picked them all up — not to mention I have no idea what the message was about because I was busy keeping them separated so they wouldn't touch each other, and I had to deal with their talking and trying to keep them quiet so at least everyone else knew what the message was about and … blah, blah, blah."

Eddie did return to the church to reclaim our adventurous child, who, by the way, had no idea he had been left. At the time, there was nothing at all funny about that incident, but in the years since, we have gotten a lot of laughter mileage out of that. I will add that this was a few years prior to cell phones, so it was not quite as easy to check with one another. Today, a quick text might solve that problem for some of you.

Sometimes it is the simple things that get miscommunicated, and we can have a good laugh. Other times our miscommunication is not so funny. It is so important to build good communication skills early on, because the longer we are married, children arrive, stresses come to visit, and good communication is a necessity. Just think about the what-ifs and the need to be able to talk openly and honestly with one another without fear of rejection or being unheard. Like, what if we have to move and we do not want to? What if the kids rebel? What if our sex drives are vastly different? What-ifs do not always come, but sometimes they do. We need to be prepared, and the more we practice good communication skills, the better we will get at it and the more prepared we will be when the big things of life land on our doorstep and we have to deal with them.

Here is one: What if our plans, the way we thought life was going to go, do not turn out like we expected? We have this image in our mind before marriage of how things will be, and then life throws us a curveball. Good communication may determine how well we deal with the unexpected turns. And building good communication over time will give us a great advantage when life is hard.

Justin shares his and Jessica's story and how they handled a major curveball in their plans.

Justin: There are these moments in life where we get the privilege to peer over the bannister of life and dream into the future, to see what might come. One of those moments happened somewhere in our early twenties. I'll never forget late-night conversations with close friends about starting families, raising men of God, and changing the world for Jesus. As you dream and pray and long for that to become reality, you start to visualize what it would look like. You start making plans with your future spouse, and conversations get more serious about how you want to form your new family.

For my wife Jessica and me, failed pregnancy test after failed pregnancy test started to interrupt our plans, leading us to wonder if we would ever have the chance to build our family like we wanted. The discouragement mounted, and the ability to enjoy the journey waned. Since we're being honest, sex became a task instead of a pleasure. I'll never forget one chilly

December day in 2016 when Jessica called me and told me we were going to adopt. She was excited. I was scared. This wasn't the view I saw years earlier when I envisioned the mountain range called home. Adoption was expensive. I wasn't prepared. My head was full of excuses, yet my heart was becoming tender. That small inkling of excitement that filled Jessica leaked into my soul and led me to chase God down on this. What did He think? Was this the path we were supposed to take? We had a different plan A, but maybe God knew better. It was a few days (or weeks) later, and I can see myself now sitting in my cubicle at work, listening to a podcast from a local pastor about the biblical family unit. I don't remember anything the pastor said, but I'll never forget how God completely melted my heart that day and gently led me to where Jessica already was: the heart of God for our family.

I love the passage in Isaiah 43:19 where the prophet speaks to God's people and says, "Do you not perceive it? I am doing a new thing" (ESV). The perceptions of the past? Forget about them. The way we thought it would appear? God has better plans. "I will make a way in the wilderness, rivers in the desert." He's inviting them into a different approach to life. They had gotten used to the routine of slavery and oppression. The familiar will always entice us away from the adventure to which God is calling us. We've all heard that perception is reality, but unfortunately, perception is merely deception if it's not connected to the heart of God for us and our families.

This is something we had to learn. *"It wasn't supposed to*

be this way" could have become our anthem. Instead, *"It's better this way"* became our confession when we aligned our hearts with God's. We believed that God wanted to take our season of barrenness and turn it into the birthing of something new. Jesus spoke of this throughout the Gospel of John, but He dug into it specifically in John 16. Jesus is trying to explain to His somewhat senseless disciples the *long game* that is playing out not only in their lives, but, in a more glorious way, in all history and eternity. Jesus knew that His purpose in life was to be the bridge that would span the gap between God and creation, but when He appeared on earth, they couldn't grasp the idea of God suffering, or that Jesus leaving them was the best option. In verses 21-22 of John 16, Jesus says, "A woman giving birth to a child has pain because her time has come; but when her baby is born she forgets the anguish because of her joy that a child is born into the world. So with you: Now is your time of grief, but I will see you again and you will rejoice, and no one will take away your joy." He also says in verse 33 something a lot of us are familiar with: "I have told you these things, so that in Me you may have peace. In this world you will have trouble. But take heart! I have overcome the world" (ESV).

Let's break that down a bit with some context. The disciples, after they followed Jesus for a while, came to the realization that He was who He said He was (Matthew 16:16, John 20:28). Some realized this before His death and resurrection; some after. They left everything to follow Jesus, so we can imagine how comforting, relieving, and empowering it was that this guy, Jesus, was the real deal. He spoke with wisdom like they'd never heard before. He did miracles that were impossible in the eyes of man. He made claims like "I am the resurrection and the life" (John 11:25). They believed, and with that belief came their own expectations of what Jesus came to do, based on their current circumstances.

At the time, the Roman Empire was in control of the nation of Israel, and the era of Caesar Augustus (27 BC – AD 14) was heralded as "good news," with Augustus being the "savior" who brought "peace." It was not a controversial subject at all for him to be called the son of god or divine one. Rome was the empire of all empires, the gold standard. So with the birth of Jesus into *this region*, at *this time*, there is inevitably going to be some clashing of heads. Luke speaks of Jesus this way: "Do not be afraid; for see – I am bringing you good news of great joy for all the people: to you is born this day in the city of David a Savior, who is the Messiah, the Lord ... And suddenly there was with the angel a multitude of the heavenly host, praising God and saying, 'Glory to God in the highest heaven, and on earth peace ... '" (Luke 2:10-11, 13-14, ESV).

The disciples had this expectation that Jesus, the true Savior, was going to overthrow the empire in power and make right all the wrongs they had experienced. This was a short-term vision that obviously comes from our inability as humanity to see outside of our own space and time. They wanted immediate relief from their problems, to be a part of this new Kingdom Jesus was ushering in.

Don't we do the same thing? [Insert problem here] + [Insert Jesus here] = [Insert expectation here]. We think Jesus should do this or do that, based on our plans or what we think is best. But we are reminded by God in Isaiah 55:8-9: "My thoughts are not your thoughts, neither are your ways my ways," declares the Lord. "As the heavens are higher than the earth, so are my ways higher than your ways and my thoughts than your thoughts" (ESV). We find a crucial lesson here for all of life: *We don't always know what's best for us.* Thank God for that. We do. Especially on the other side of the miracle. At the time, like the disciples, we find ourselves asking so many questions, and wondering if there's any purpose at all to what we're doing. This leads us to the next lesson: *Where God is, there is purpose, peace, and provision.* We may not understand why it happens the way it does, but we must trust that God does.

We believe through Jesus' words in John 16 that the pain and the process are so important, because without it nothing of significance can be birthed. When we step into this belief, we start to see that God always meets us there. And in this way, does the statement, "It's not supposed to be this way," shift into the belief that, "It's better this way"?

God's way for our family is the best way. Yes, we must make plans. We must chart a course and move toward it with meaningful action. But the decision we've made as a family is that we will write our plans in pencil and give God access to the eraser.

We pray that your pain won't be wasted for any reason, but that from it will come something beautiful. We pray that you will respond to trouble with rejoicing and perseverance. We pray that you will lay your family at the feet of Jesus and follow His lead. We pray that you wouldn't just confess, "I will follow you wherever you go," as did an onlooker in Luke 9:57 (ESV). We pray that you would obey after your declaration and do whatever Jesus says, even if it means walking away from everything that is comfortable, right, and good in your life.

From our experience, and the experience of millions of other believers for thousands of years, we can truly say, in whatever circumstance we find ourselves, "It's better this way." We now have two boys that we couldn't imagine life without. They are the apple of our eye and an everyday reminder of the beauty amidst the pain.

EDDIE

Genesis 2:25 talks about being one. We always think in terms of the physical, and it is, but it is so much more than that. Adam and Eve were naked, they were open, they were transparent. There was nothing hidden — no secrets, no shame. Being one means we are on the same page. And yes, sometimes getting there is a journey. But good communication with one another and listening closely to Jesus, wanting what He wants for us, makes marriage beautiful.

Men, maybe this is more difficult for us. Studies of newborns reveal that females move their lips much more than males. A study on preschool children reveals that almost 100 percent of the sounds made by girls were word-related, but that was true only sixty-eight percent of the time for boys.

Thirty-two percent of the sounds boys made were mere noises — grunts, as well as airplane, truck and gun noises. Some women might say their husbands have not advanced much. Women tend to be better communicators. They are right-brain oriented. They focus on emotions, feelings, creativity. Generally, men are more left brained — logical and analytical.

The point is, we are different. And we have to work at this. We cannot be lazy; we have to be willing to communicate. We want the marriage to win at all costs, and good communication habits lead to a win for all.

When we prioritize communication with our spouse, other areas of our relationship grow as well. Friendship is an extremely important part of marriage. Friendship is built around communication. Do you want a more intimate relationship with your husband or wife? It begins with communication. I am not just talking sexual intimacy. I am talking about the intimacy of truly knowing one another. Intimacy is defined as close familiarity. Emotional, mental, spiritual and physical intimacy are all needed in a healthy marriage, and most of it is born and bred in how well we communicate with one another. In fact, it is important for us men to understand that intimacy, to a woman, denotes mutual vulnerability, openness and sharing. You cannot be in an intimate relationship with someone, in the truest meaning of the word, without healthy communication.

"Marriage is an attempt to solve problems together which you didn't even have when you were on your own." — Eddie Cantor

Chapter Five

Just keep doing it …
Under the covers …
Or anywhere else, for that matter.

"Sex without love is as hollow and ridiculous as love without sex."
— Hunter S. Thompson

DAWN

Sex. Why is that a word that makes middle school kids giggle and adults get the deer-in-the-headlights look? Why do we parents get sweaty palms and a racing heart when our children/teenagers ask questions about it? Why do the most laid-back personalities go into a full-blown panic attack when the subject is broached?

Maybe the only thing harder than writing about it is talking about it.

But why? Why is something as amazing and wonderful as sex so hard for most of us to talk about? Or write about?

Sex is a healthy desire given by God to us as a gift, but it is meant for marriage. God is not anti-sex. He created our bodies for sex, a gift meant for pleasure and enjoyment. There should be no shame in it.

However, many of us who grew up in church, in an effort to keep us pure, might have received the message that it is dirty and shameful — something we do but do not talk about. I am not blasting the purity movement. We stressed purity with our children, especially as they walked through their teen years. But purity is so much more than "do not have intercourse." It is an attitude. It is the way you carry yourself and present yourself. It is what you think about and what you talk about. Purity is as much for married adults as it is for teenagers. Unfortunately, through the years, we have equated purity with virginity only, and we have sent so many mixed signals. And the biggest mistake we have made is choosing silence over conversation and projecting shame over beauty. So we have sent not only mixed signals, we have sent the wrong message.

For others, the shame may come from a place of having been used or abused. You were victimized, but made to feel guilty, like it was your fault. You have lived life believing sex is harmful and hurtful. And now, even though you are in a married relationship, sex is still about shame, and nothing to be enjoyed.

We have been told by people that sex and intimacy is not a subject that should be preached. There have been complaints when a youth pastor has dared to talk about the damage of pornography to students — not because they did not agree, but because "it shouldn't be talked about in church."

So if the church should not talk about it, who should? If the church and the home are not the safe places for this discussion, where is the safe place? Where do children and teens go for honest conversation about such an important part of life?

It is easy to think that it was just a time long ago that sex was a taboo subject at church, but we have heard those same arguments and complaints in recent years.

I had a young married woman in her twenties reach out about this very thing. She grew up in the church, a godly young teenager and now a young married woman, saying that she was totally unprepared when she got married for a healthy sexual relationship with her husband.

So whether you are our age or much younger, you may say the same thing.

I struggled early on in marriage. Sex was actually addressed fairly well in the student ministry I grew up in. My mom, unlike my dad, was somewhat easy to talk to about the subject. However, I did not go into marriage with the healthiest of views.

I met Eddie when I was sixteen years old. We married when I was nineteen and he was twenty-five. We had the same belief system, so we waited until we were married to have sex. As a nineteen-year-old who grew up in church, knowing sex was fine once you were married, I still had this hang-up: Why is it suddenly okay just because we went through this twenty-minute ceremony? Is there anything that is off-limits even though we are married? (Because I had heard from various resources that certain things were still wrong.) Add to that the fact that Eddie had been with someone else before we met, and I plunged deep into the comparison trap. Would he like it with me? Would I be enough for him? How will I, do I, compare to the other? Will he, does he, think of her? Come on, girls, you know what I am talking about. We are the worst when it comes to comparing ourselves, and especially in the vulnerable places, the places we feel the least equipped. I definitely did not enter marriage in the healthiest place in that regard.

We did not want children right away. I had never been told that sex was as much about pleasure as procreation. Maybe people around me believed it, but they never said it. And our premarital counselor did not mention it. I think what helped me, along with reading some books that were boldly written from the Christian perspective, was that my husband was older and had a greater understanding of biblical marital sex.

I do not know about you, but I grew up where, if someone was outspoken about sex, it was from the standpoint that some things were sinful even in the marriage bed. I do not remember any Scripture being quoted, maybe because there is no Scripture to back up that opinion … in my opinion. Sadly, that continues to be an opinion for some today and is still taught in many places.

My hope is that this chapter will be honest and bold as we look at healthy marital sex from a biblical viewpoint and point out some dangers when boundaries are not in place.

EDDIE

I was definitely not raised with healthy conversations

when it came to sex. I remember my dad trying to talk to me and my response being, "Yeah, yeah, Dad, I know." I basically blew him off, like many teenagers. When I was in high school, he handed me a box of condoms and told me, "If you are going to do it, you had better use these." And that was the beginning and end of my sex education, other than the locker room, and the movies with friends I should not have watched.

Dawn and I both want this to be a chapter that is helpful, and we believe that in order for things to be helpful, they must be transparent. We will not shy away from terms or experiences that brought us to this point. We will not cover up past mistakes or issues that we struggled with, all in hopes that it will help people we know who are struggling in this area of their relationships. We were told of one statistic that claims sixty-six percent of married couples have some kind of sexual dysfunction. That is two couples out of three that you know. That dysfunction could be the result of medications, hormones out of whack, past regrets or shame, trust issues, etc.

I am amazed at the number of people who want the "no strings attached" sex. So many people of all ages want sex without all the emotional attachment or commitment. Is that even possible? I don't think so.

We were with one of our sons at the JUCO World Series when he was playing college baseball. There were people who served as hosts to the teams. They would sit with their visiting team to cheer and offer help. Many would have their team over for cookouts. The point was to make the teams and their families feel welcome in the city. The lady who was our host took her duties seriously. We overheard her conversation with one of the dads on the trip. It went something like, "My husband is away this week, and when he is out of town, we have an understanding. He's given me a 'hall pass' this week, so would you like to come over?" That invitation was not meant for the entire team and their families. That was a personal, one-on-one invite.

Apps like Tinder have turned up the volume on this hookup culture, the no-strings-attached sexual encounters. And we have no clue yet as to the long-term effects of Instagram and Snapchat or even text messaging. Proverbs 6:27 in *The Message* says, "You can't build a fire in your lap and not burn your pants."

DAWN

I don't believe there is any way of disconnecting your emotions when you have sex. They may not be healthy emotions, but emotions are involved. Sex done right is something we should look forward to and be excited about. The Bible is not shy about sex. In case you didn't know, there is an entire book in the Bible dedicated to the sexual relationship. Read Song of Solomon sometime. Talk about bold writing. Sex is a gift from God, and He always gives the best gifts.

Compare Song of Solomon sometime to what a twenty-nine-year-old was quoted in *Rolling Stone* magazine regarding his definition of sex: "Sex is a piece of body touching another piece of body — just as existentially meaningless as kissing." Does that viewpoint get anyone excited about sex? Does that cause you to see it as a beautiful act between two people? Not me! I want all the emotion, all the feelings of connectedness, the full-blown experience with someone you have all the feels for. The idea of just body parts touching does very little for me. But, then again, I am a woman. And other women may have a differing opinion.

EDDIE

Sex and intimacy are not the same thing. You can be married for years and not experience intimacy. One of the issues with intimacy is some people talk about intimacy as "I am into me, you see." That's not true intimacy. And when that is your idea of intimacy, you will have issues. God created sex for unity, pleasure, and procreation. It was His idea, and it was a great idea.

Mark Driscoll, in his book, *Real Marriage*, says, "We only had fifteen minutes between teaching sessions at a marriage conference to say hello to people and expected that perhaps a few would come up and introduce themselves. Instead, they lined up more than a hundred deep to drop the bomb of their sex lives on us in a minute or less. Women who were molested as children, weeping so hard they could not breathe; husbands who had been caught, yet again, viewing porn; a married couple who had not had any sexual contact in more than a decade; a woman who had sex with her husband twice a day and was still unsatisfied, wanting more; a few couples who had been married more than a year and were still virgins; one woman who had not told her husband she had dozens of partners before they met; a wife who asked if her husband was guilty of raping her; and a Christian couple who wanted to know if they should keep watching porn together. And those are just a few of them."[8]

Lovemaking is an honorable activity. It is not dirty. It is not gross. It is not a necessary evil. So the problems are in our minds and attitudes, how we were programmed. The key is to see sex as God does, something to be avoided outside of marriage, but to be enjoyed within.

DAWN

Before we jump into healthy married sex, which is where we want to focus, let's deal with two things that can hinder it.

Let's talk porn.

Did you know that the average age of viewing porn online is eleven? Did you know that the largest consumers are boys, ages twelve to seventeen? Did you know that the mean age of first-time intercourse is 16.4?

I do not know about you, but those are frightening numbers to me. And what is even more frightening is that the church is not speaking to this. Too many parents are not having conversations with their kids. At some point we have to get past the awkwardness and talk. We have to be willing to have the hard conversations. Do not think that porn is just a teen problem. It starts there, but it creates an addiction that leads into adulthood and is a huge problem in marriage. While we have kept silent, it has crept into our marriages, Christian and non-Christian alike. That problem is sitting on the pews of every single church today, and not just in the pews where the students are sitting. And not only the pews, but standing behind the pulpits, as well.

Porn is hard to avoid in our culture. Addressing it will take intentionality.

EDDIE

Pornography is the largest epidemic among men, but it is fast becoming an issue for women, as well. Porn is fantasy. You have these well-endowed physical specimens performing without any issues. For a man, it is just easy. He does not have to worry about pleasing her. There is no fear of rejection. There is no work involved. It is just easy and selfish. No one can live up to what they see on the screen, and, unfortunately, for many of our kids, that is where their sex education is coming from.

For those married couples struggling with this issue, let me say a few things.

First of all, you are not alone! There are many in this boat with you.

Forgiveness, respect, trust, and love will be the keys to getting through this. Forgiveness is something you will have to choose daily. It does not make what your spouse is doing or has done right — forgiveness makes you right. Respect will come. Changing what you think will change how you feel. Your love can be stronger than their weakness. It is a head-hands-heart thing. Change how you think. Use kind words and touch. And your heart will follow. Trust will come over time, but you cannot start here. The average amount of time to regain trust is about two years. Trust is the foundation of love. When you feel safe and vulnerable and strong in the relationship, that is when you will know that trust and love have returned.

DAWN

There is so much more that could be said when it comes to pornography, and it is not a simple 1-2-3 plan and all is well. Seek counsel. It will probably take that for both of you to survive this monster.

Let's talk about something else that does tremendous damage to marriages: infidelity.

Affairs are orchestrated by Satan himself. All Satan needs is a tiny crack, and he can destroy us. None of us should think we are above it. Kyle Idleman says, "The journey to the pigpen almost always starts when we minimize our sin."[9]

How many times have we heard, "It just started with ..."? It always starts innocently. Know this: Flirting with anyone other than your spouse is NEVER harmless.

And let me add, sex is not the only thing that should be reserved for your spouse. There are certain looks, pats, hugs, etc., that should be different between the two of you. Reserve those things so that they mean something.

We recently were with a group of ministers and their wives. I stood and watched with amazement — and, honestly, disgust — as one of the wives worked the room, hugging or walking by and touching every man in the room while her husband stood back. Later, as we were in a session, I watched her stroke her husband, but what I normally would think of as sweet and affectionate, I thought of as ordinary, because she had basically acted that way towards every other man in the room. It had lost its sweetness.

Before we close this out, let me add, because sometimes we girls are as bad as the boys with this, do not share intimate details of your relationship with others. Not even your best girlfriend, ladies. That is bringing others into your relationship as much as porn. Save some things for the dignity and value of your spouse. You may think that goes without saying, but believe me, I have been on the receiving end of information I would rather not have heard.

EDDIE

Here is something to think about: If the strongest man, Samson, and the wisest man, Solomon, and the holiest man, David, were all vulnerable to sexual sin, then so are we. Just let that sink in. No matter how strong we are spiritually, or think we are, we need to be on guard.

The tragedy of David's affair with Bathsheba and the consequences that followed are played out over and over again in society today. We reap what we sow. There will be a payday. You can mark it down. God may not settle His accounts in thirty days, but He will settle them. When we are careless in our behavior, it will lead us down a path of destruction.

What causes affairs?

So often it is just emotional immaturity. I know a man

who left his wife, saying he wanted to date other people. Date other people. Like he was in high school.

Sometimes you have a man who is used to being the big man on campus, thinks he is God's gift to women, and after being married a while is not getting stroked like he wants, so he looks elsewhere. Or you have a woman who was popular in school, and maybe Daddy gave her everything she wanted, and now she is having to live on a budget and it feels like she has no life.

Another thing that can lead to affairs is unresolved conflict. DO NOT EVER talk to the opposite sex about your marriage problems unless you are talking to a counselor. The reason that other person is easy to talk to is because you do not have problems with that person. If you married that person, you would be having the same problems with them, or similar ones. She is probably dressed up and fixed up and smells good, while your wife is at home pulling her hair out with preschoolers. Or maybe he is kind and says all the right things because he does not know how needy and nagging you really are.

What about unmet needs? Men and women both were created with some basic emotional needs. The need for affection, attention, and acceptance are a few. Most all affairs begin with some type of emotional attachment. Adultery starts in the head long before it gets into bed.

If you have tried talking about these unmet needs that you have but there is no change, try meeting a need that the other one has. Give it time. Do not quit too soon. See if perhaps when you focus on your spouse's needs that your needs do not get met as well.

Unfulfilled expectations also get people into trouble. The marriage has not turned out as expected. One or both of you feels cheated, and bitterness sets in. We feel entitled; we feel like we deserve better. And we meet someone who feels like they deserve better, as well. Talk about a setup by Satan himself.

I mentioned how affairs start in the mind. Undisciplined thinking gets us into trouble. We are fed a constant diet of immorality through what we read and watch. It affects our thought life. James tells us that as a man thinks in his heart, so is he. What you think will eventually determine the way you act. Philippians 4:8 tells us to think on things that are true, noble, right, pure, lovely, excellent, and praiseworthy. Perhaps bring your expectation level down to a place of reality and then think on the ways your marriage is lovely, even excellent.

Lack of boundaries is dangerous and can hang us out to dry. Do not spend time alone with the opposite sex. I do not ride in cars with women alone. I do not meet in my office with women unless my assistant is in the next room. I do not counsel women. Set boundaries in your life that you and your spouse can live with. Boundaries may look different based on many elements. But everyone needs boundaries. Talk about those that you can both function within and feel comfortable and secure with.

I have told my wife before that one of my life goals is to be able to look at her before I go to be with Jesus and say, "I've been totally faithful to you." Come to the point where infidelity is never an option because you know that it is never worth it. Your spouse deserves better. Your children and grandchildren deserve better. Faithfulness includes physical and emotional faithfulness.

The story is told of Ali Hafed, a wealthy ancient Persian who owned much land and many productive fields, orchards, and gardens. He had a lovely family and at first was contented because he was wealthy, and wealthy because he was contented.

An old priest came to Ali Hafed and told him that if he had a diamond the size of his thumb, he could purchase a dozen farms like his. Ali Hafed said, "Will you tell me where I can find diamonds?"

The priest told him, "If you will find a river that runs over white sands, between high mountains, in those white sands you will always find diamonds." "Well," said Ali Hafed, "I will go."

So he sold his farm, collected his money that was at interest, and left his family in charge of a neighbor, and away he went in search of diamonds, traveling through many lands in Asia and Europe. After years of searching, his money was all spent, and he passed away in rags and wretchedness.

Meanwhile, the man who purchased Ali Hafed's farm one day led his camel out into the garden to drink, and as the animal put his nose into the shallow waters, the farmer noticed a curious flash of light in the white sands of the stream. Reaching in, he pulled out a black stone containing a strange eye of light. Not long after, the same old priest came to visit Ali Hafed's successor and found that in the black stone was a diamond. As they rushed out into the garden and stirred up the white sands with their fingers, they came up with many more beautiful, valuable gems. According to the story, this marked the discovery of the diamond mines of Golconda, the most valuable diamond mines in the history of the ancient world.

Had Ali Hafed remained at home and dug in his own cellar, or anywhere in his own fields, rather than traveling in strange lands where he eventually faced starvation and ruin, he would have had "acres of diamonds."[10]

What a sad story that is, we may say, and it is. But how many do this very thing every day — maybe not in search of diamonds, but in search of something that, if cultivated, they would find right under the roof of their own home? The problem is we always think that under our roof is where the problem is and that our happiness is out there somewhere. And we walk away from the riches God has blessed us with that can be found right in our own home.

DAWN

If some of us would spend the time working on our own marriage that we spend trying to build and hide illicit relationships, the divorce rate would be lower and our marriages would be much happier. If some men, and women, would flirt with their spouse the way I see them flirting with others in the coffee shops and gyms, their sex lives would be on fire. Satan will always show us the good and cover up the consequences. He provides opportunity when we are at our most vulnerable.

That is why, as Eddie said, it is important to have boundaries in place that we will not cross. They protect us. Ask yourself if it is really worth it. Is it worth losing my spouse? Is it worth the heartache it will cause my children? There are a lot of costs, and many of the costs show up years down the road. Just as I would say about porn, I say about those off the screen: Stop looking at someone who does not belong to you! Stop having intimate conversations with someone you are not married to. Keep your hands to yourself. Sometimes just a few basics can keep us out of a world of trouble. Be careful out there. The world, and the Enemy, have no boundaries.

EDDIE

People do not like to hear this, but when you got married you gave up the rights to your body. That being said, this is not a license for abuse. That would be perverted, ungodly and sinful. God's way is always about "What can I give, how can I best meet your needs and desires?" Most every couple has some kind of issue when it comes to sex, whether physical, physiological or psychological. Studies reveal that it takes the average couple five to six years within marriage to make the adjustments needed, and many go through their entire marriage with sexual problems and issues unresolved. But do not give up. Hang in there. Communicate with each other.

Some couples fall into the trap of manipulating or controlling one another by withholding sex. Sex is never to be used as a weapon — a tool or a reward. According to 1 Corinthians 7:5, the only time you should abstain is when you mutually agree for a time of prayer and fasting. Okay, and how many really do that? I'm sure very few for the purpose of prayer.

We are busier than ever, but we make time for things we really want to do, for the things that are important to us. Sex is an important part of marriage. We need to talk honestly and do it often. Make time not just for the "act" but for lying next to each other, cuddling. I know, guys — some of us do not really need that, but she may.

Sometimes quickies are necessary, but it should not be like that all the time. I know if there are kids in the home, it can be tricky. You may not have a lot of time or energy. Get creative. If possible, get away together. Have a date night. If you say you cannot afford it, think about all the things you spend money on that are unnecessary. Dawn and I used to do date lunches, and when kids are in school you have the house to yourself. (Hint, hint!)

Safeguard yourself with a vital, vibrant sexual relationship. The grass is not greener on the other side. Water your own grass. Make it so green that all other grass will look brown.

DAWN

Did you know that twenty percent of couples who stay married have sex ten times a year — or less? That scares me as much as some of the other statistics we have talked about. I love what Levi Lusko says in his book, *Swipe Right: Life, Death, Sex, and Romance:* "Now yells louder, but later lasts longer."[11] Satan knows when to strike with comfort sin. And that's true before marriage and during marriage. Louis Giglio says, "They

131

don't make a condom that fits over your soul." How true is that?

One of the ways that the Enemy blinds us and messes with us is to not only encourage us, but set us up with opportunities to have sex before marriage. And then, once we are married, he keeps us busy, preoccupied, maybe even disgruntled, enough so that we do not have sex. He is crafty, friends. Intimacy is a brilliant weapon against the Enemy. His game is to divide and conquer, to destroy us. Our spouse is our only legitimate means by which we fulfill one another's sexual desires. Talk honestly, and do it often. Having sex with our spouse is ALWAYS a good decision. It strengthens the bond between couples. It is a powerful gift.

I can tell you that after my mom died, it was the closeness I needed. I did not initiate it, but I remember Eddie initiating it and saying, "You probably aren't in the mood for this right now, are you?" I was not in the mood, but I knew I wanted the closeness, and it turned out to be exactly what I needed. It has tremendous healing power in hard times.

Eddie may correct me here, but I do not remember ever refusing him. I remember saying, "Later," at times, but I do not remember saying no. I mean, he was fine with our four kids and ten of their friends in the room next to us. He was fine if I had been cleaning the house or was just finishing a workout and smelling of sweat. Me, not so much. So sometimes, my response was, "Can I just get a shower first?" or, "Can we just wait until everyone is soundly asleep?" And then there were times, like Eddie has said, that a quickie was appropriate, as long as it was quiet. I can tell you that at times I consented begrudgingly, from a wrong attitude, or too busy, or people in the house, or ….

I know, at times, that I went through the motions, but I can promise you I was always glad that I consented. Remember earlier my mentioning some of the things Eddie and I had fought about? Sometimes it is a fight to have sex. I get that. We can always find a reason or excuse. But that is a good fight to fight together. Fight for it — together.

Sex is one of those things we have never had too much of an issue with (other than, as I have mentioned, getting past some of my programming early on and rejecting the comparison trap). We had issues with time; we have four kids, after all. We had issues with being too tired; remember, we have four kids. Stress played in at times; sometimes that was because we have four kids. Other times, just the normal life stress we all face. I got pregnant easily, so I vowed abstinence after our third child. It lasted about six weeks. You guessed it, postpartum was it for the abstinence. Just remember that it is worth the fight. Get creative. Get some vitamins. Turn off the TV. Turn off your phone. Go to bed early. Just do it. The more you do it, the more you will want to. Use it or lose it.

EDDIE

Communication is a huge part of intimacy. How do you actually do something together that you cannot even talk about? Do you ask your spouse how he/she likes it? Do you ask what turns him/her on? Most of the communication between couples, if any, seems to be "Can you do this for me?" or "I like it this way." Focus on your spouse and what pleases them, and you will find mutual satisfaction in marriage. You may not like a certain thing, but if it pleases your spouse, at least try. I have had friends who would say they liked and wanted certain things, but they were unwilling to do things their wife wanted. That does not work, friends. Be sensitive to one another. But you have to talk. You cannot read each other's minds.

Ray Ortlund says, "If you don't learn what makes your wife tick, then you will only discover what makes her ticked."

Another thing to mention that causes a struggle at times is baggage. We all come to marriage with a certain amount of baggage. It may be different types, but it is all baggage. Sexual baggage could include belief systems, how one was raised, mistakes made in the past, hang-ups. Those are all things that would be best discussed before marriage, but so often they are not, and so they show up afterwards. Those are things that can be worked through and solved, but they require communication, as well. Communicating with each other builds intimacy. It leads to the physical closeness, even spiritual closeness. It binds our emotions together and creates oneness. That is one of the reasons sex gets better with age and the length of time two people are married. Hopefully you have learned one another and you have spent time talking. You never stop growing, so you never stop talking. What you may have enjoyed ten years ago could look different now. That is okay. Just keep growing together and trying new things.

All the problems already mentioned can be solved with good communication and understanding, and that includes being honest and transparent, even vulnerable, with each other. If you feel like you are in a rut or bored, talk about it. Get away, even for a night, just to change the scenery.

The beauty of married sex is that you have an entire lifetime to work on it. I remember friends asking me before Dawn and I were married how we would know we were compatible in this area if we waited until we were married to have sex. You do not have to be compatible on the honeymoon. You have an entire life ahead of you to get to know each other in this area. Do you want to know why sex gets better with age and the longer you have been married? It is called life experience. Teens and twenty-somethings sometimes think that those are the best years for sex. They could not be more wrong. Sex gets better as intimacy grows. And intimacy grows as you live a life together. Life experience breeds intimacy, and intimacy breeds great sex. Dawn and I have birthed and raised children together and then watched them leave to live their own lives. We have moved to different places and set up life and ministry together. We have survived the stressful years of preschoolers and teenagers together. We have mourned the death of grandparents and all our parents together. We have faced loneliness together and, through that, developed a friendship with one another that goes beyond any other friendship or relationship. We have faced loss through the physical death of friends, as well as the death of friendships due to betrayal. We faced hurt and felt the sting of our children leaving for college, as well as the bittersweetness of them leaving us to cling to their new spouse. Life done well together is fertile ground for intimacy, and that gives growth to some of the greatest lovemaking that only God could create.

All of this is what sets the married relationship apart from all other relationships. Protect it. Fight for it. It is worth it.

DAWN

Okay, let's get practical.

Ladies, I am going to direct my thoughts to you and leave the men to my husband.

First of all, if you have not gotten the message from us by now, God is all about us enjoying sex. He created us in a way to enjoy it. Not to give a science lesson here, but you do have a particular part that has no other function other than enjoyment.

The second thing is this: NO ONE has the moral authority to tell a married couple what they can do or not do. We will tell you the things that we believe to be off limits, and why, but we hold to the belief from Hebrews 13:4 that the marriage bed is to be undefiled. That simply means that the marriage bed is to be kept pure, and sexual intimacy is reserved for a husband and his wife. The marriage bed is the safest and most sacred place.

In light of those two things, the questions that usually arise are, "Are there boundaries?" "What is allowed?" "Is it okay to experiment?" "What about different positions, toys, fantasies, oral/anal sex?" Most of the time, I think these questions come from a place of fear — fear of being sinful. If that is true, here are a few questions to ask yourself and explore as a couple: Does the Bible forbid it? Does it violate my spouse? Is it safe physically? Could it cause harm if we're not careful? And will it damage our relationship?

Ladies, we carry a lot of power when it comes to sexual intimacy. In the routine of life — with trying to work, to mom well, be a good wife, serve our community — sex so often can become another thing on our to-do list. And many times we fail to check that one off. Can I tell you that men take that rejection very personally? Keep that in mind, along with the awareness that he does not perceive you as just tired, or just stressed. He perceives that you do not want him. And none of us enjoy that feeling. If we could remove the word duty and replace it with desire, we would be better off. If the desire is not there, pray for it, if you are a believer in prayer. I can tell you that I have prayed that prayer, and it works. I have found that when it comes to lovemaking, the more you engage in it, the more you want it. Surveys have been done, and married men with a strong sex drive who are denied tend to border on depression. If you are a single woman, here is a secret: Save sex for marriage, and then make up for lost time! (That goes for men, as well, but I am directing this to women, remember?)

I have found in talking to couples that one thing most every man says he wants is for his wife to be the initiator more. I know, ladies, it is not my strong suit either. I used to say, well, if I initiate, too, it will be happening every day. That was my cop-out. Not good. Everyone needs to feel needed. It may not be on our radar, but it is on theirs. Everything does not have to be perfect. All the laundry does not have to be put away; the dishes do not have to be done. The entire house does not have to be clean. And you do not have to be just stepping out of the shower. All those things are on my list of excuses, as well. Eddie knows I hate to be sweaty when he is in the mood, and I never have understood why that does not bother him. Just one word to men: "Chore-play" — offering help around the house, helping with the kids, maybe even running the vacuum occasionally — is a form of foreplay, so helping out with the aforementioned might improve your sex life.

And then schedule it, if you must. We schedule everything else, especially what is important to us. You may prefer spontaneity, but real life happens. Scheduling can also help us plan for it and look forward to it. Mindset plays a role for us, right, girls? It may help get us there faster if we have had some time to think on it.

Girls, I also know the struggle of body image. We all have that. We all have insecurities. I wish I was five inches taller, with legs for days, but it is never going to happen. Can I tell you that most husbands do not care? They want us, extra pounds and all. And, unfortunately, they want to see. They are visual creatures. I like the lights off; Eddie wants them on. I say dim lighting is a good compromise.

Can we talk kids and teenagers in the house? Remember, we have four. We have faced all the sticky situations that can add or detract from your sex life. From low libido caused by exhaustion, nursing babies, and being pregnant, to the fear of being caught. And yes, we have been caught. We survived it, and so will you. When ours were little, it was hard to have a conversation, let alone a lovemaking session. (Some may argue that point, seeing we had four children.) You actually do make time for things that are important to you. And it was always very important to both of us. But, honestly, I was super fertile, to the point of not wanting Eddie to even look at me. I will tell you that our kids did have early bedtimes so that we had several hours in the evening to ourselves. And when they were teenagers — well, that is when the lock on the door came in handy. And they never quite learned that the lock also meant do not stand there at the door knocking, calling for Mom — always for Mom. For some reason, they never called for Dad. But, again, that never seemed to bother Eddie. It totally took me out of the game.

There is a time and a place for quickies, but do not let that be the norm. Make it an event, when possible. And that may take scheduling, depending on your season of life.

And like Eddie said, you have to talk. You may not want to have those conversations in a restaurant where you have eavesdroppers or at home where there are antennas everywhere, but find a place and a time, and talk. You have to be willing to say what you like and do not like, what your needs and desires are. He wants to know. I think most men really do want to please. They just sometimes need a little guidance.

EDDIE

How true is the saying that men are like microwaves and women are like crockpots? And why did God make us so different?

Foreplay definitely starts in the morning, guys, if you want your wife to be ready in the evening. It is amazing what a text just to check in during the day can do for you later. Helping around the house and with the kids will all work to your advantage (not that that is our reason for doing it, I am sure). But if you want it to take less time when you get to the bedroom, start early.

Dawn is right, I have never talked to a group of men who did not express the desire for their wives to initiate more. Men, learn how to make your wife the best version of herself. Pursue her heart, and she will initiate sex more. This goes back to communication, but talk about how often you both need to have sex. What would you both agree to being a healthy number? Sex is a determining factor to how healthy your marriage is. It is not the only factor, but it is an important one. So talk about what your needs are, and come to some understanding about how often it should happen. And then, especially if there are children under the roof, come up with a game plan to make it happen. Maybe even set up a number of how many times each should be the initiator during the course of a week.

Maybe it is another form of foreplay, but talk is key, especially for women. Emotions tie in, and for men, they are more likely to talk after there has been sex; and for a woman, she is more likely to have sex after there has been some talking. Again, God made us different, but the adventure it creates is amazing. Enjoy the differences. Improve your communication skills, men, and you will improve your sex life. Again, we are very different. I know God has a sense of humor, but it is also good, because it makes us work for those things that are important to us, and to work together.

Another difference is that for many women, the less they have sex, the less they want it. It is just the opposite for men. The less men have it, the more they want it. This is not true always, but most of the time. Sex may not be on women's radar for stress relief, but it definitely is for men.

Make dating your spouse a priority. That does not end when you get married. And you do not have to spend a lot of money. We did not have a lot of money for that when we had a young family. But, like Dawn said, we put the kids to bed early. And when they are teenagers, tell them to go to their room and do not come out until morning. They have plenty to keep them busy in their rooms. For us, sometimes we talked, sometimes we watched our favorite show or a movie. Now we have Netflix and Hulu. But do not let those things, and your phone, steal your time together. Quiet is good. Order in pizza. We used to run the bathroom fans after we put the kids to bed to drown out our conversations. Now, of course, there are sound machines, but, again, you do not have to spend money. Most bathrooms have a sound machine built in.

Do not forget the sensual, in place of the sexual. There is a difference. Sensual involves cuddling, hand holding, saying things. And not to just lead to sex. I know, men — again, we may not need these things, but she does.

Our spouse is the most sanctifying relationship we will have. Sex exposes our selfishness. It takes the average woman ten to thirty, or even forty-five minutes to move from foreplay to orgasm. Stop being lazy, guys. Put in the effort.

And, as Dawn already said, yes, we are visual. Help us out, wives. Dawn and I have compromised on the light issue. Wear what he likes for you to wear. Do not always be covered head to toe at home.

Dawn has covered what we believe to be allowed between married couples, so let me add a few questions to consider. Ask if it is a violation of Scripture. Ask if it is helpful. Ask if it will pull you together or push you apart.

There are only two things we would say are off limits, if you cannot guess. One is porn. That should have no place in the relationship, whether together as a couple, or as individuals. It does a lot of damage — not only to the relationship, but to your brain, as well. It is bringing someone else into your relationship and causing you to lust after another. And it probably goes without saying, but in our culture may need to be said: absolutely no threesomes.

Marriage is like a savings account. The more you invest, the better the payoff. That includes our sexual relationship. Sex done right is to be exalted. It is not dirty or gross. It is not just to have babies, but to bring fun and excitement and pleasure to both. At one time it was portrayed as something women just had to grin and bear. Not true.

In closing this out, let me say, if you are not married, do not rush into marriage. Take time to get to know one other. Get to know how each other responds to stress. See your potential spouse when they are angry. Observe their character in different situations. Get to know that person, and save the sexual relationship for marriage. It will be worth the wait.

Whether you are married or single, if you would say that you have messed up already, remember: God is the redeemer of all things! Trust Him to give you a fresh start.

The best marriages are those in which two people are looking out for the best interests of each other, serving one another, and are committed to one another for the long haul, no matter what.

"You should be kissed, every day, every hour, every minute."
— *Nicholas Sparks,* The Lucky One

Chapter Six

Man up.

"Any man who says he totally understands women is a fool, because they are ununderstandable." — The Office

EDDIE

Wow, that sex chapter was long, so now I have a dilemma. I need to say a lot to us men. This should probably be the longest chapter in the book. With that being said, I realize how short our attention spans are. But I also realize we will make time and space for what is really important. And second only to our relationship with Jesus is our relationship with our wives. We can all stand some growth and improvement in this area — in fact, both areas — but we will deal with our relationship with our wives for now.

When we apply for our marriage license, all we do is pay a fee. There is no job description available. There is no training available. We just pay a fee and we get a license. How easy it is to get married. If only it was that easy to stay married. Maybe if we had to work a little harder to get married, we might work a little harder at staying that way. As a pastor who performs the wedding ceremony, if I fail to mail the license in, I pay a fine. After thirty-plus years of marrying folks, I have never neglected to do that. Yet, I must admit, that after thirty-plus years of being married to Dawn, I have often neglected some things. I have neglected some of her feelings, her thoughts, her needs. If I made that my lifelong habit, I would pay for it in much greater ways than a fine — our marriage would suffer untold harm. I am still growing, still learning about her, still figuring out what makes her tick and what makes her ticked. It is a lifelong process. She continues to throw me curveballs occasionally, but that keeps things exciting and very interesting. So wherever we are on the marriage journey — ready to get started, or years in — we can always improve. Again, apart from our relationship with Jesus, what relationship is more important than the relationship we have with our spouse?

Now, I understand that everyone reading this is not coming from a place of faith, so some of this may not make sense. It may seem foreign, and you may totally disagree. That is okay. I would encourage you, however, to continue reading. Perhaps you will be open to the possibility that God's way may be worth exploring a little deeper.

I have found, even after thirty-plus years, that I still need to turn to God's Word as my operations manual when it comes to marriage. It is timeless and up to date. It has been proven to work. The passage I refer to and try to live by is Ephesians 5:25: "Husbands, love your wives just as Christ loved the church and gave himself for her" (NIV). I do not see a 1-2-3 formula or five specific things I should do or not do. Simply, love your wife the way Christ loved the church.

So let's look at that. How exactly did Jesus love the church? Sacrificially. All right, then. I know that is not simple. In fact, it is quite the challenge. It is a verse we would rather ignore, or at least overlook.

We know the preceding three verses (Ephesians 5:22-24). Those are the "wives submit to your husband" verses. We have memorized those verses. Problem is, we have misinterpreted and even perverted those verses. It does not mean to rule over, or to be better than. In fact, it is hard to have that kind of attitude if we are sacrificing for our wives and putting her needs above our own.

In terms of these verses, here is what we really need to grasp as husbands: We are equal. Remember, we mentioned before, God took the rib from Adam's side. From Adam's side! As the old Rabbi said, "God did not take a bone from his foot that he would walk on her, or from his head that she would walk on him." (I would add, or from his neck that she would be a pain.) You get it, right? We are to be co-laborers, side by side. She would complement him, and he would complement her. In fact, God said she would complete him. You are not complete without her.

Yes, it is a challenge to love your wife the way Christ loved the church. Most men would say, no, that is not a challenge, it is impossible! So, why even try? It is a little bit like "turn the other cheek" when someone punches you. Yeah, that is what Jesus did, and I know that is what I am supposed to do, but I am going to punch you back. That is because we live reactionary lives. Instead of being Spirit-controlled, like the Bible says in Ephesians 5:18, we are reactionary, like someone who is drunk. We react according to our carnal nature.

When I was in college, I worked with a man older than I was. And we drank on the job. (Yes, I know, I should not have been doing that; but just so you know, I was legal at the time, but still no excuse.) One day he got cute and pulled some hair off my chest. Out of reaction, I punched him in the chest. That is how we so often operate in marriage. We react and punch back. Our wife says something that pushes a button or sets off a trigger, and we punch back. She does something that makes us mad, or wounds our ego, and we punch back. Maybe not with a tight fist, but with a sharp tongue. Because that is what we do; it is how we live.

Ephesians 5:25 is impossible to fulfill unless we have fulfilled Ephesians 5:18. We must be Christ-centered. My life, my marriage, my job should all revolve around Jesus. We cannot compartmentalize our lives. We cannot live reactionary lives. As believers, His Spirit fills and leads us. We have His nature and the power of the Holy Spirit within us. So, then, we really have this capacity to love our wives the way Christ loved the church.

Let's try and keep it simple. There are two main points in Ephesians 5:25 concerning the role of the husband. And, if we are Spirit-controlled, we can fulfill the command to love our wives as Christ loved the church. Scripture tells us that we are to lead and we are to love. I have heard many pastors, teachers, and counselors say, "Husbands are to be loving leaders." Yes, lead, but be loving in our leadership. Too many husbands abuse and misuse their leadership. Often, it turns abusive and they abuse their wives and children mentally, emotionally and physically. They somehow have the twisted and perverted idea that they have that right. Give some men a little authority, and it goes to their head. They are large and in charge and rule over their home like a tyrant, always insisting on their own way. Leading without loving leads to tyranny. I am not real smart, but I am smart enough to know that my wife has better judgment than I do in many areas of life. I lean on her, she leans on me; we are equal.

Jesus is always the best example of a loving leader. He had infinite power, yet He led in love. I had a theology professor say that you could describe Jesus as "love in the form of a servant." He was God! Yet, He loved and He served. That is how Jesus loved the church and gave Himself for her. He sacrificed His very life.

Making sacrifices in order for love to rule your marriage is not always comfortable, but marriage in its very essence is about sacrifice, about serving, about getting out of our comfort zone. Think for a moment with me about Jesus. I do not think He was comfortable on the cross. And, yes, do not forget that He had the power to leave. He could have come down from the cross. He could have walked away. But He chose to stay because He loved us with a sacrificial love. That is what He chose to do. I am sure He did not feel like staying. In addition to the physical pain and emotional suffering, there was the spiritual torment when He, who knew no sin, actually became sin. That is something we cannot relate to. But I am glad

He stayed. I know you know where I am going with this. So often when our marriage faces difficulties, when the going gets tough and uncomfortable, too many men decide to leave, to walk out. "Well, I just don't love her anymore. My feelings have changed. This marriage is tough. My wife doesn't act the way I think she should act. She isn't the same person I married. I'm just going to leave." I am thankful Jesus loved us enough to stay. (I know that there are plenty of women, as well, who walk out and leave their husband and children. It is not always the husband who chooses to leave and break up the family. I know that serving one another and sacrificing for one another goes both ways, but let's focus on us as husbands, at least in this chapter.) Sacrificial love is when we give ourselves for our wife's well-being. It means being selfless and putting her needs above our own. And, for those men who claim Ephesians 5:22 as their life verse ("wives, submit"), love your wife like this, and she will have no problem being submissive.

"But, Eddie, you don't know who (what) I live with. She does not deserve it." Again, keep in mind the comparison here. The husband is to love his wife the way Christ loved the church. Do we as the church deserve His love? He loves us in spite of our faults. While we were sinners, ungrateful and rebellious, unloving and disloyal, Christ made the sacrifice for us.

Let me ask a question. Is the church always submissive to Christ? Is the church (I am talking about the people, not the building) often critical, judgmental, and hypocritical? Do we often act one way in church (or at home) and another way when we are away? Are we not a needy people, quick to complain and find fault? Do we not have ungrateful attitudes where nothing ever seems to be enough, no matter how much God blesses us? We are tight-fisted when it comes to giving and serving, yet we live with open hands in terms of wanting people to give to us. We have this "give me more, do more for me" kind of attitude, and yet God continues to bless us and love us. Jesus loved the church and gave Himself for her.

Husbands, I encourage you to take the lead. Choose to love your wife the way Christ loved the church, with a sacrificial love. Often, your wife will respond to that love, and the relationship will be stronger than ever and better than you could ever imagine. Sadly, some will not respond. For some, it is never enough, no matter how much we try or how much we do. When men tell me it is not going to work, I will always say, you want to do all that you can, and then some, because you want to look back and say that you gave your best, that with God's help you gave it all you had. Your wife has a free will, just like people in church have a free will and sometimes walk out on God.

All marriages begin with potential. But do you know the definition of potential? As a noun, it means the possibility of becoming something. As an adjective, it means showing the capacity to develop into something. So all of us, when we get married, have the potential within us to make something of our marriage. The question is, what will that something look like? It really comes down to who we are willing to follow and whose blueprint we will use. If we both are sold out to Jesus

151

and follow Him and use His blueprint, there is great potential for our marriage not only to survive, but to thrive. It is worth the effort.

No marriage is perfect. All marriages have issues. To say the contrary is either to lie, or you have not been married very long. No, you would be lying. To be married any time at all is to realize that it is a challenge.

The Enemy wants to wreck your marriage and he is very skilled at doing so. I have heard men say from time to time, "I just can't make her happy." That is not your job. Your job is to make her holy (Ephesians 5:26). To make holy means to set apart and declare as sacred. It means to elevate and lift up. We are to love with an elevating kind of love. While you cannot make her happy, I can assure you that when she is holy, she will be happy. That is a byproduct of holiness. Sir, your wife will be more satisfied and fulfilled because of your lifting and elevating love. Real love lifts up, it never drags down.

A few questions to regularly ask yourself: Am I lifting my wife up or dragging her down? Is she better because of me? Am I drawing her closer to God or pulling her away? Does she feel cared for? Noticed? Needed?

Maybe some wives would say they feel *too* needed. Wives are not intended to be our mothers, guys. They should not have to treat us like children and do everything for us. But I know they do want to feel like they are needed as an equal partner walking through life with us. May we love our wives in an elevating way that meets her needs and desires and draws her closer to God.

Someone said, "Too many marriages are like a tick on a dog. They are locked on for all they can get out of it." Also, in many marriages, you have two ticks and no dog, and they just suck the life out of one another.

This lifting, elevating, sanctifying love honors our wife and presents her in all her glory (Ephesians 5:27). Yet, for too many wives, the opposite is true. They are blemished because they have not been loved well. Have you ever met a man who does not satisfy his own needs and does not take care of his own body? When his body needs rest, he rests it. When it's hungry, he feeds it. When it's dirty, he washes it. Most men take care of themselves. I know some do not, but that is rare. That is not the norm or the natural. He is going to care for himself.

I never knew that I had an eye problem. Well, if I am honest, I did know, I just did not want to deal with it. I did not go to the doctor for regular checkups when I was very young, so I never had an eye test. I knew I could not see very well, but it was all I knew, and so it was normal, at least to me. When I was in school, as well as enduring athletic physicals, I would cheat on the eye chart. I would memorize what the person in front of me said. I knew I had a problem, but I did not want to wear glasses. Back in the day, glasses were not cool, and kids were just as cruel as today. Later, when I began wearing contacts and then glasses, I was at an age where glasses made you look smart (and cool). Wow! I could see! I did not know what I was missing.

I also never knew that I had an "I" problem. I was totally

blind to that. When it comes to marriage, most of us are not aware of the tremendous "I" problem that we have. The "I" problem is camouflaged by other problems many of us believe we have, and probably do have. However, the "I" problem is our greatest problem and possibly our most dangerous problem. Most of us men would concede to problems in our marriage, such as finances, communication, sexuality, career pressures, in-law struggles. These are all problems that we struggle with, but for me — and you may say, for you as well — my biggest problem is me.

Isaiah 53:6 nails it. The verse says, "We have all turned to our own way" (CSB). I want MY way. We get caught up on the "acts" of sin. Sins such as murder, adultery, lying, stealing are all acts of sin. They are the fruit, but the root is selfishness. It is the attitude that "I want what I want, when I want it, because I want it." We are sinful, and we commit selfish acts in order to get our own way. We can write it in big, bold letters: SELF.

Back in the day, when I worked with Fellowship of Christian Athletes, we had a booklet we gave to people who made decisions for Christ at FCA Camp. This was not unique to FCA, of course, but in the booklet was a drawing that looked like a throne, and the throne had a capital S on it. In everyone's life there is a throne. For the person who does not know Jesus, self is on the throne. When a person trusts in Christ, Christ should be on the throne. The problem is, because we are selfish, even after we become followers of Jesus, self wants to dethrone Jesus and climb back on the throne to be in charge. That is why I must die to self, and I must die daily, perhaps several times a day. I must continually die to my own desires, my own wants. But I want to be happy and I want what is best for me. It is just hard for me to let go of control and allow Jesus to rule and reign, even knowing that is what will truly make me happy.

Again, Isaiah 53:6 says, "We like sheep have gone astray and turned to our own way." If we are not careful, we will act like the sheep and go astray. Sheep look for greener grass, and they always believe that it is greener on the other side of the fence. Selfish independence seeks to fulfill myself. Put that together with another person just like that, and then add children to the mix, all seeking to live for self, and we have constant conflict.

The key to a healthy marriage and a happy home is a Christ-centered life. Gentlemen, we must take the lead in this. This is our responsibility. We are the ones who must set this tone in our homes of seeking to do things Jesus' way and keeping Him on the throne in our homes. A me-centered life will never bring satisfaction, purpose, or fulfillment. When Jesus is at the center (and on the throne), we care about our spouse. We love like Jesus and want what is best for our spouse. We love like Christ loved the church, and that is a sacrificial love. That is where we really find meaning and purpose. Is it problem-free? Of course not. But we eliminate the biggest problem — SELF. And it cannot be, "Well, if she will, I will." It has to be, "I am going to take the lead with this" and then we pray that our wife follows our lead. If not, we still love with a sacrificial love.

A loving husband will care for his wife's needs and desires and will seek to satisfy her. Yes, that means putting her needs and desires above our own. The problem is, most husbands do not love their wives enough to know what their desires are, much less seek to satisfy and fulfill them, which means we need to learn our wives in order to meet their needs. Dawn told me just the other day that when the children were small that I would gladly do anything she asked me to do. Problem was, I had to be asked. Remember reading what Kaylin wrote about our son Stephen? I passed that gene along to him. I am a "nine wing one" on the Enneagram personality test. And if you know anything about the Enneagram, then you know that a nine is never quick to jump into a situation. They do not always see what needs to be done, or if they do, they do not feel like they can offer anything of value, so they just observe. I did a lot of observing. And sometimes nines are just oblivious. That does not mean I can excuse myself. I need to work on that. I am just saying that is how I responded. I was oblivious to what was going on right before my eyes. I thought the house looked great, the cooking was under control, and the laundry never seemed to pile up. The kids were always healthy and cared for. Everything was under control. I did not see anything I needed to contribute. Dawn had it all under control, and managed. I failed to recognize the stress she was under trying to keep it all together. Should she have said something instead of continuing to plow through? Yes. But there were things that I could have taken off of her just by being more observant and more compassionate. When we fail to study our wives and learn them, we create stress in our marriage. I know it is a challenge. My father-in-law, who just went to be with Jesus, said, "I'm eighty-three years old and I still can't figure out women." And sometimes when we think we have our wife figured out, she changes on us. I get that. But maybe our perspective needs to change so that we see that as interesting and challenging instead of frustrating.

Men, do we love our wives enough to learn them? It is worth it! Learn her love language, and then speak it. That language may change over time, but that is a woman's prerogative. Dawn's love language was Acts of Service when we had four children at home. Now, with an empty nest, it is more Words of Affirmation, and Touch. And while we are thinking about love languages, I have an issue when we just focus on that. My wife's love language may be Words of Affirmation, but that does not mean that I never buy her gifts. That does not mean that I do not intentionally spend time with her.

An important part of this is also realizing that your wife is different from you. In spite of what the transgender agenda would say, she is different. As we said earlier, which bears repeating, studies of newborns and small children reveal this. Experience reveals this, as well. I saw it in my children, having two girls and two boys. I see it in my grandchildren. Females are much more vocal. They speak earlier and more often. (Watch it, men.) Little boys just grunt and make noises like cars, trucks and planes. (Not much changes, does it?) When my daughters were little and wanted some juice, they would say, "Juice, please." My boys would point at it and grunt. Women tend to be better communicators. They are more detailed and creative, being more in touch with emotions and feelings.

As a general rule, but not always, men tend to be more analytical and logical. Men tend to just hear words, without meaning or feeling. Has your wife ever said, "Don't just hear what I say, listen to what I mean"? Yeah, that confuses us men. It is like reading the paper, or being on the phone or computer, or watching television, and your wife is obviously upset. You ask, "Baby, what's wrong?" She responds, "Nothing, I'm fine." So we go on with what we are doing, when everything about her — body language, posture, expression and tone of voice — says otherwise. Men, hear more than words. Love your wife well and learn her.

Yes, learn her language. Gary Chapman's great book talks about the five love languages: Quality Time and Words of Affirmation, Gifts, Acts of Service and Physical Touch. Again, don't neglect the other four, but do major on the one. Hold her hand, give her hugs, put your arm around her. Jesus touched people. Speak softly and say, "I love you," as often as you can. Praise her in private as well as in public, especially around other women. Help her! Don't let your wife be like the woman who entered her husband in the "most useless household gadget" contest. Date her. Take her out to lunch or dinner. Get away. Spend time together. Dawn and I love being together. We love cruises, the beach and the mountains. But most of all we love being together.

Thomas Carlyle, the great writer, historian and mathematician, wrote in his journal after the death of his wife, "If only I could see you once more to let you know how much you mean to me, how much I really loved you …. You never really knew." Let her know, men. Tell her and show her.

For wives who may be reading, please know I do not believe that most men set out to be emotionally distant or lazy. We want to please, and we understand the need women have for attention and affection. We understand the need women have for emotional security and that most often that is one of your greatest desires, maybe even more than financial security. We just do not always know how to arrive at that place of safety for you.

Being a good husband is subjective. What does that even mean? I do know that the better we know ourselves, the better off we are and the better off our wife should be — that is, if we are willing to make necessary changes to be a better man, rather than excuse our way out of everything.

Here are a few questions to ask yourself, just to do a little self-inventory:

What do you think you should do better?

Does my wife get the best of me, or do I give her leftovers?

Is the overall atmosphere in my home centered on me and what makes me happy?

Do I practice non-sexual touch?

Am I her biggest cheerleader?

Do I help out at home, since I actually live there too?

Am I quick to say I am sorry, and do I forgive quickly?

Do I share my dreams and plans with her?

Do I treat her like she is my best friend?

Do I hear what she is saying — like really listen — when she talks?

Bottom line, ask your wife how she would answer these in reference to you, if you are truly brave.

So we have been told what we are supposed to do, how we are supposed to act, what we are supposed to prioritize, how we are to lead and how we are to love. The problem is never that we do not know, the problem is actually doing the thing. There is so much pressure and stress involved in leading our homes, making a living and making a life. We come into our marriage with so many expectations and desires. The problem is that our wives come into marriage with their own set of expectations and desires, and those do not always line up together. The challenge is in how we can bring all those together so that they become our desires, instead of his and hers. It is a challenge, and it does take time, a lifetime for most of us. It takes work, but when we are willing to do the work, to step up to the challenge, we have much happier and healthier marriages. There is no denying that women are different. But are we not happy about that? I know I am.

I know all this is not that hard. It is really impossible. Jesus was God incarnate, after all. To love your wife the way Jesus loved the church is a huge goal that we will never totally arrive at, but a goal worth pursuing, striving to make some progress. But let us end where we started. There is no way you can fulfill verse 25 (love your wives the way Christ loved the church) unless you have fulfilled verse 18 (be filled with the Spirit). All roads lead back to Jesus and being Christ-centered. When Jesus is the center of our marriage and our lives, we can lead and love like Him. Actually, He will just do it through us.

"When you look in her eyes and she's looking back in yours, everything feels ... not quite normal. Because you feel stronger and weaker at the same time. You feel excited and, at the same time, terrified." — Superman

Chapter Seven

Between Us Girls

"The trouble with some women is that they get all excited about nothing — and then they marry him." — Cher

D A W N

I wish we could sit down, one on one, and chitchat. I am not much for small talk, but I love to hear people's stories — where they came from, who influenced them most, what their belief system is and how it was born. If I could, I would take you to my favorite coffee shop; it is new wave and quaint, and they welcome young hipsters and young mamas and older mamas alike. I would get my favorite barista, who happens to be my son, to fix you your favorite coffee drink. Mine is either the seasonal one or my never-fail go-to, *tres leches*. I think you would love it even if you are not a coffee drinker.

We would sit in my favorite spot, the one my husband and I usually share on Friday afternoons, and I would probably pepper you with questions about your life, because that is kind of what I do best. Some may call it nosy. I call it interested. Maybe it is a little bit of both. I am pretty transparent. I will answer any question as honestly as I can. Nothing is off the table. But I will respect you for not being that way. I love spending time with women of all ages. I believe we are all extremely interesting, with different likes and opinions and takes on the world. We all seem to come to the coffee shop with our own set of issues, a certain amount of brokenness, a sense of trying to appear to have it all together and at the same time knowing that we are all messed up, just to different degrees.

Many of us have struggled with insecurities that continue to haunt us, wondering if we are enough. Are we enough for our husband, or is there something more he needs? Will he love us forever or eventually want someone different? Are we good enough moms that one day our kids may actually like us and call us friend? Are we good enough sisters and daughters that we are needed, even if only for our presence? Are we good enough friends? Pretty enough? Fit enough? Smart enough? A good enough cook that people want to dine at our house?

Many of us have been used and abused by strangers, and even people we trust. We have been looked at as though we have nothing to offer in a boardroom or a bedroom. We have been abandoned by friends, by husbands, by fathers. And somehow, with all of that against us, we have made it work for us. Or God has. He has created these stories of triumph, even if short-lived. We have gone from victory to victory. We have clawed our way out of some pits of our own making or the pits we have been thrown into, and we have lived to tell about it. We manage our households well. We run million-dollar businesses. We parent one, four, six children, some of us as single parents. We hold down forty-plus-hour-a-week jobs. We return to school, maybe while we have a job and family. We travel and minister all over the world. We offer aid to victims of sex trafficking. We serve our local church, community, neighborhood.

And with all that, sometimes we still struggle to know who we are. Not all of us, I am sure. I do, at times. I've worn so many hats at the same time and still wondered, "Who the heck am I?" Daughter, sister, wife, mom, mom-in-law, granddaughter, Gigi (that's my grandmother name), chauffeur, referee, nurse, counselor, tutor, teacher, dog mom, event coordinator, cook, maid — and those are titles I had within the home. Throw in friend, small group leader, pastor's wife, business owner, coach, room mom, women's ministry leader. I am Eddie's wife, Chrissie, Jessica, Stephen and John Michael's mom. I am Michael, Justin, Kaylin and Noelle's second mom. I am Gigi to Brooklynn, Mackenzie, Addison, Ezra, Jed and Jaxon.

I have all these titles, and had you asked me who I was, I would have given you a title or how I belonged to one of these aforementioned people, but no clue who Dawn really was. How does that happen? It happens so often because we get caught up in performance, the things we do that appear to make a difference to others; we judge ourselves based upon the world's standards and culture's chart and forget that it's not about any of that.

God says we are His daughters; that makes us daughters of the King, and it is not based on what we look like, how we act, or what we do. Now can we all take a big breath together and exhale? Feels good, does it not?

So for the next little bit, let us focus on our lives as wives.

If we are sitting together at Methodical Coffee enjoying our *tres leches* or a pour-over or espresso, and I asked you what you wanted or expected from marriage, what would you tell me? Would you immediately begin to tell me what you want your husband to do for you? Would you tell me how your husband could meet this need or that need and make marriage better for you? Would you begin to unpack for me all the expectations and desires you carried with you down the aisle and into your new life?

Here's the truth, girlfriend, with a ton of love behind it: We need to work on us. We have zero control over our husbands. We have great influence, but we cannot control them, or anyone else, for that matter. What if he never changes? What if he never does that thing we think we need him to do so badly to make us happy in marriage? What if he never makes the income we thought he would? What if he never gains victory over that bad habit, that sin, that addiction? Will you stay? Will you cut and run? Is there any scenario where you would say, "If this happens or doesn't happen, I will leave the marriage"? (Again, I am not talking about any type of abusive relationship. If you are in an abusive relationship, I would encourage you to seek counsel and do what you need to do to be physically safe, as well as emotionally and mentally healthy.)

I love social media, maybe too much. I hasten to say that I am *so* glad we did not have it when our children were small! I hate to think of the time I would have wasted on it and the things I would have missed if my face had been in my phone as much as many young parents today. And the feeling of documenting everything instead of just living, and my pride winning to the point of me posting every detail about my children, and do not even get me started on the comparison it breeds. For someone like me, with my insecurities, I would have always felt like I played not just second fiddle to everyone, but I would not even have been in the orchestra. No, thank you!

I love Instagram, because I am a picture-crazy person, but it does us no favors! It is the best of everything. It is beautiful even when it is not, thanks to filters and all that jazz. Homes are always spotless. Children always act perfect in videos and look their best in pictures. I have raised four. I know that is not real life, and I know it does not help others when we act like it is. I know what real picture-taking looks like with four kids. It usually amounts to threats and offers of treats "if everyone can just smile and look this way at the same time," and "the sooner we get this picture taken the sooner you can go back to yelling at each other and strip off the cute clothes and put the dirty ones you love back on," and "for goodness sakes STOP TOUCHING her, and you stop picking your nose," and "move this way so all that garbage spilling on the floor does not show, or the laundry piled on the couch." That is real life, friends. You know it. I know it.

So how about we just get real. I will be real with you if you will agree to be real with yourself as you read this. And since the coffee shop is a relaxed, inviting kind of place that breeds honesty without judgment, we will just pretend we are there. Together. And let's talk about how I am doing as a wife and how my marriage is going, how we got here and where we are going. And let's talk about how you are doing as a wife, how your marriage is going or maybe where you want it to go and how we can all get there. I believe one of the best ways we do that is to live backwards. Simply meaning, how do you want things to look down the road, ten years from now, thirty years from now, when the little ones turn into teenagers, when the teenagers leave home and it is just you and your hubby again? If we live backwards, then we will be intentional about doing some things now that will get us there. We need to know how we want things to turn out.

Let's just start with ongoing points of conflict. We talk about conflict and problems and fighting well in another chapter, so we will not dawdle too much here, but think about what your points of conflict are. It could be one, or many. What we hear so much are things like money woes — not enough of it, or how do we agree how to spend it. What about time? Not enough couple time or family time. Too much time at work or away. Sex is always one, but we do not seem to want to talk about that. We assume that the argument is usually from the man and it is about the lack of sex. But so often the woman complains about that as well. Or maybe it is just selfish sex or "sex is all he/she seems to want" kind of argument. Exhaustion due to speed of life, raising children, job demands. Communication or lack thereof. Lack of affection, respect, friendship with spouse. And then there are trust issues due to infidelity or presumed infidelity, jealousy, pornography, or threatening relationships outside of the marriage. Believe it or not, the list goes on and on.

What about the list of things that can threaten our marriage or at least make it more difficult? The marriage is stagnant, the phone and TV time, things are boring for one or both. Putting others (even children) before each other, we ignore problems and warning signs. The silent treatment, no sex, spending more money than we have, threats of divorce or leaving, keeping secrets, which leads to lack of trust.

Do you see what we are up against? Do you see why it is impossible to waltz through marriage and it be Instagram picture perfect? Do you see why, as much as some may want you to think they have the perfect marriage and family, they absolutely do not?

Glance back at Haggai 1 with me. It is a tiny little book near the end of the Old Testament. I know it is a weird book to go to when we are talking about marriage, but hang with me.

Haggai is a book about how the temple in Jerusalem lay in ruins, and Haggai is calling God's people to remember the things of God. Haggai reminds us that indifference towards the things of God reveals that our hearts are far from God. Enemies and everyday life have distracted God's people from what God had called them to do.

Ahh, you starting to track with me a little bit?

Stick with me here. Haggai 1:7 says, "The Lord of Hosts

says this: 'Think carefully about your ways'" (CSB).

Hmm, make sense now? Where in all of life do we need to think more carefully about our ways than in our marriages, within our homes? Statistics are against us. Culture is against us. You may not be a risk taker, but if you choose to get married, stats and culture say that is a big risk.

So let's think about our ways and how they will affect our end game.

Do we not pursue everything in building up our own homes and gathering stuff? People work longer and harder, even working several jobs. More women work today than ever before. And this is absolutely NOT a word against working women! I have my own business that I work online from home. I am just saying we need to check our why and our attitude for doing it. If it is all about "stuff," maybe priorities are a little skewed.

I remember when my mom died and we were helping my dad clean out some of her things. It was an all-day job that took our entire family, and we did not even scratch the surface. And then when my dad died ten months later, it took weeks to get the house cleaned out. I cannot begin to tell you the loads of things we gave away. We had ministries come with trucks and get stuff. That was after the entire family of kids, grandkids, nieces and nephews went through, getting things they wanted. And then, all the stuff we put on the road to be trashed — even the neighbors came over to ask if they could go through the stuff we put by the road. I stood there and thought to myself, (and out loud, as well), "This is what it comes down to."

None of this stuff even matters now. I got some things that I loved and wanted to save that had been in our family for years, and they do mean a lot. Some things would mean nothing to anyone else, but they do to me. I remember telling some family members who were standing in their house, "At different times I would think I love this piece or that piece, and I knew one day it would be mine, to share with my brother, of course, but now I do not even want it. I just want my parents back."

Honestly, only the memories really matter now. I want to remember what their voices sounded like when they talked or laughed. I want to remember every single thing they taught me, and the vacations we took, and the holidays together. I want to recall the stories my dad would tell; he was such an amazing storyteller and the funniest person I ever knew.

My mom died from Alzheimer's, and it was a long, grueling, ten-year journey. The last five years, she rarely knew who I was, and so I probably had five years to mourn her. I remember my dad saying the worst part was just watching someone who had been so vital and contributed so much in her life just waste away. My dad died suddenly. I went to his house to meet him for our standing Wednesday lunch, and I found him on the floor of his kitchen. That is just how fast things change. I had talked to him the Sunday before and planned our Wednesday together, and then, in a moment, he was just gone. That was so much better for him, but the loss we all felt was huge.

I am just trying to say that, in the end, stuff matters very little. It is the relationships and the memories we make along the way that matter. Those are the things we do not lose in the blink of an eye.

So do our ways — how we spend our time and energy and money — reflect what we say is truly important?

People got things out of order in Haggai's time. They were focused on stuff that did not matter and neglected the things that God said matters.

Our marriages are important to God. He takes them very seriously. He ordained the home before church and government. It matters to Him how we treat one another, how we live together "in the holy estate of matrimony." Did your wedding ceremony include that line? Mine did. Marriage is a holy estate, not to be entered into lightly. That hits me every time I attend a wedding.

I have already told you that I was nineteen and clueless when I got married. I knew marriage was holy and sacred, and I was absolutely certain, unlike anything else in my life, that I was to marry Eddie Leopard. The way he came into my life could not have been orchestrated by man. He was a twenty-two-year-old senior at the University of South Carolina, playing football and baseball, when we met. I was sixteen and a junior in high school, two hours up the road. We met on the football field. He was running before practice, which he never did. I was in town just for a few hours. See what I mean? I will not share our whole story, but suffice it to say, I knew God brought us together; His hand was all over it. But in marrying young, we both had a lot to learn, and we learned a lot the hard way — about each other, and marriage. Thankfully, we were both strong believers; we knew going in that this was it, no way out.

I say all that to say this: Even though God was all in it, over it, and around it, and we knew it, marriage was not, and is not, easy. It is not easy for anyone. Two imperfect, selfish people under one roof is never going to be easy. But it has been good. It has been great, in fact. But I will share this with you, too.

I know the exhaustion of raising young children. We had four, age six and under at one time. We did wait three years before having children, thank God, but after that, somehow we lost control, as if we ever had it. In case you do not know, you do not have nearly the control you think you do when it comes to having children. We had our daughter and three years later our second daughter, and we thought, "This is perfect." Three years seemed to be the magic number to wait, so that was our plan. God had other plans. Fifteen months later, our first son arrived; nineteen months later, our second son made his entrance; and one year after that, after a scare that number five was on the way, my husband went to the doctor with my blessing.

Those four would grow up to be teenagers. And they really were very good teenagers — but they were teenagers. It was stressful. It was busy. The house was noisy. Eddie worked a lot and also traveled a lot. He was busy with a growing and thriving church, and he was busy with outside commitments. I was a stay-at-home mom and I loved it. It is all I ever wanted to do, but it was also lonely and isolating at times. We lived away from family, and some days were nothing more than pity party days for me. Eddie came home one day and into our bedroom to find me curled up in a chair, in a fetal position, crying, proclaiming I was just too tired for this anymore. We did need to reevaluate some things, and we did. I was struggling with "Who am I?" and he was struggling with "What am I supposed to do about it?"

To think I ever struggled (actually, I struggled constantly) with the idea of an empty nest is hilarious to me now. But when you do not really know who you are outside of someone's mom and all the titles that come with that, you start to wonder what life will look like, be like, when it happens. We had such a dear godly friend who constantly said to me, "There is life after children." I do not know why he said that to me so often. I think he, in his godly discernment, knew I needed to hear it. And he was right.

Pity parties, money woes, communication problems, time-management problems. Yep, we had them. Every day is not a goosebump day. Some days Eddie would come home and I would say I had to go to the store just to get out of the house. Alone. I cooked dinner so many days with a baby on my hip, one wrapped around my leg, and two under my feet. And guess what? You guessed it — I would do it all over again in a heartbeat. Yes, it was hard. Yes, it was exhausting. But it was good — REAL good — as one of my grand girls likes to say.

Sometimes, girls, it just takes grit and determination. I am sad to say, sometimes I do not see enough of that in people today. We have gotten soft. We have become entitled, spoiled. Some young couples have told us, "We just want to start where we left off." What took their parents twenty-plus years to get, they want when they return from the honeymoon. It does not happen like that, at least for most of us. We have to work for things, and we even have to work at our marriages. They do not just happen. It takes work. It takes faith in God and in one another. It takes digging deep, most days. It takes choosing him, choosing her, every single day. And most days it takes just plain grit.

My very first mentor, who entered my life when I was about eighteen, used to tell me that it took more than the shallow kind of love to make marriage last for the long haul. She said most of the time it means "hanging in there." She reiterated that to me recently when we were together at her husband's funeral service. They had been married for sixty-eight years. I asked her what she would say to a young bride sitting across from her today, and what should I say to them. She said, "Tell them the same thing I said to you: 'Just hang in there.'"

So that is a glimpse into my story, just so you will know that we did not walk through fields of flowers on seventy-degree days, with the sun shining every day, for over thirty years. There is no way you can be married that long, with four children, without going through a lot of stuff and a lot of tough days. Just remember that as we continue this discussion.

So let's talk men for a moment. We are not going to male bash; I deplore that! But we need some understanding, if that is even possible, into the male psyche. I still need all the help I can get. I have a husband, two sons I birthed myself, two sons I get to share (thanks to my daughters marrying well) and three grandsons (at the moment). And they are all different. Just when I think I have them figured out, they change it up on me, including my husband. But it keeps things fun and adventurous, right?

Here is what I know from my own experience — my research — as well as from talking to many and asking a lot of questions:

Men want:

More than almost anything, respect. Did you know that eighty percent of men need to know that we believe in them, that they are able? In that same survey, it showed that eighty percent of women need to know that they are lovable, beautiful, that he notices her. So if that is you, know, then, that as important as it is to you as a woman to be noticed and seen as beautiful, for men, the respect and belief in them is that important.

And I don't mean just saying we respect them; they need to see it. How do we do that? I believe it usually comes in the things that we say. How do you talk about your husband when he is around and not around? I recently listened to two young married women talk about their husbands as we were laying out next to them on a cruise ship. They complained about everything: what time he got home from work (instead of praising him for working), how slow he ate his dinner (instead of being thankful for the time to sit there together). And you may say, well, the men were not there to hear it. True, but if that's how they feel, trust me, their husbands know. They did end the conversation with, "I do love him though." I thought, "Really?" No, I did not say it. Maybe I should have.

What about phrases we use like, "Well, I knew that was a bad idea," "I knew that would never work," "I tried to tell you," or "I told you so." Yikes! And the tone of voice!

Disrespect also happens in the form of sharing too much information with others. I've heard some women share some intimate details with girlfriends before that left me wide-eyed and blushing. No, I am not a prude, but it left me thinking that locker room talk does not just happen in male locker rooms. Some things are just personal and should be kept private. No one needs to know all the details.

Men also want the nagging to cease — that constant griping or complaining about the same thing. I know what you are thinking, I have thought it too: "If he would just do it when I asked him to …." I said that often to my kids, and that is allowed! Husbands do not like it too much, ladies. "A nagging wife is like the dripping of a leaky roof in a rainstorm. Stopping her is like trying to stop the wind. It is like trying to grab olive oil with your hand" (Proverbs 27:15-16, NIRV). Oh, boy, heard that. None of us want to be characterized like that. Treating them that way is called parenting. We do not need to parent our husbands.

And then there is sex. We asked our small group of young marrieds one day when we were studying sex (yes, we actually do that), what was one thing the men wanted more when it comes to sex. I know, dangerous question, right? Every single man said they wanted their wife to initiate more. They want to feel wanted and desired too, ladies. I'm proud to say many came back later saying they were making the effort. Funny how it takes effort, is it not? But it is so true: Satan will do everything he can to get us to have sex before we are married and everything he can to keep us from it when we are married. We have a whole chapter on this subject, so I will not tarry, but sex is extremely important, and it needs to happen often! As John Eldridge says in his and wife Stasi's book, *Love and War*, "You need to do it. Often. In a way you both enjoy it. Immensely. If this isn't the case, then you need to deal with why it isn't. Cause you need to do it. Often. In a way you both enjoy it. Immensely."[12] Very good advice!

Men want time to unwind. We hear it all the time! Men do not want to walk in the door and in the first ten minutes hear everything that went wrong that day, how little one needs Daddy to dole out some discipline, that the faucet is still dripping and the dog peed on the carpet — again. Give them some time; set the stage a little. Timing is everything.

And then they want to hear, "Thank you." I know, so do we. But if we can try to avoid that feeling that says, "He never thanks me for all I do," we will be better off. It may even rub off a little bit. Just do not be afraid to be the one who initiates the kinder, gentler way. As hard as it can be, do not just expect him to help with the children. Not all of them are wired that way. Eddie was always willing to help with anything, he just never saw for himself what I thought needed to be done. I did not want to have to ask, either, but they just do not always see things like we do. And avoid saying, "Thank you, but you should've done it this way," or "Thank you, but you shouldn't … ," or "Why didn't … ." Just leave it at, "You done good." Otherwise, they hear, "You tried but failed." Remember, one of those needs they have is being believed in.

We were in a restaurant, and it was crowded and congested, and it was a serve-yourself kind of place. We watched a man tell his wife to sit down and he would get the food. He came back with barbecue, and when he sat down, without hesitation, she said, "You didn't even get any sauce." His entire countenance changed.

It is true, they are different from us. Men can be more task-oriented, and women can be more about the journey. Ever been shopping with them? Sometimes they want to get in and get out, while we just love milling around. Women are constantly wondering if he still loves us, and for men, they feel like they settled that when they married us. Women still love to date, and men may marry thinking they never have to date again. Men need applause; maybe we women do, too. Everyone needs to feel like the one they love most is cheering for them. We all need to hear that what we do matters and that we do it well.

This may not be true for all, and certainly we do not put all men and all women in the same boat and say this is how they are, because it is not. And after saying all that, and the statistics about men, let me say this:

Stop trying to figure out all men, and start figuring out

your own man. My man does not fit into every statistic. He is not like all men when it comes to how he feels about things or how he sees things. Thank God for that! He is not like "all men," and I am not like "all women." We cross back and forth and zigzag all over those lines at times. That is not a bad thing. It is a good thing. But it is why we need to study our own spouse and learn them, as well as give room for growth and change. Praise God I am not the same nineteen-year-old he married. He is glad of that, too. We are all changing and growing in many different ways. My husband is unique. Different things make him tick, and different things make him ticked. My mindset is, there is no way I am starting over with someone else. I have too much invested here. We need to all be about tending our own garden and staying out of others.

Here is something to think about as we grow and age: If your husband is tall and thin, then you are into tall and thin. If your husband is short with an athletic build, that is what you are into. If he is blond, you like blonds. If he is fifty, you no longer like twenties. And the same for men. I know from research that men tend to have a little more difficulty with this, which may tend to be a reason some of us women are a bit insecure. Research shows that women seem to like whatever their husband evolves into with age. For instance, if he used to have a head full of hair, but now he is fifty and bald, she now likes fifty and bald. Men tend to think back to what their wife looked like when they met, and want that. Not to scare anyone, but it is what it is. That probably goes along with men being more visual, but it is no excuse, gentlemen (in case you are reading this chapter), for any kind of indiscretion.

Since we have said that we have zero control over our men, let's focus on us. What are some things we need to embrace, change, tweak, work on, that will make us better wives?

Let's go ahead and address the elephant in the room. I feel like you know it is coming. I don't know why we dread talking about it. It is like a dirty word, so maybe together we can clean it up: the "S" word — not sex, but submission. Okay, we said it. Again, deep breath, exhale.

This is not going to be so bad, I promise. It is actually quite freeing. It puts the pressure on the men and takes it off us, if we can just yield to it. Before you start telling me how your personality goes against it and you cannot help it, blah, blah, blah, let me tell you that it is not within any of our personalities to do this. I am a control freak in every way. Most of the time I trust my own instincts. I believe I have very good discernment. I believe I do things the right way, otherwise I would do it another way. Anyone else? So, when Eddie and I do not agree on something, obviously I think I am right because, well, of all that I said above.

I also come from a long line of strong, independent women who struggled with submission, as well. Not to speak ill of my mom, but she very well could have been queen of strong women. (Shh, don't tell.) One of the things I remember my mom saying (her way of excusing herself) was that Dad was just very laid back and her personality was "take charge," so she "had to." She would say, "I wish he would, but ...." Umm, no! Here is the deal for all those who would fall under my mother's way of thinking: If you want the man to step up, stop occupying the space! I believe I first heard that on a podcast, and when I did I was convicted, myself, but I thought of my mom. Oops. I know we are not supposed to do that, but we are being honest here, so that is what I honestly thought.

Ephesians 5:22 introduces us to the principle of submission, and it is one of the most misunderstood and misused passages in the Bible. The world rejects it. Christians fight over it. Some compromise and say it is ancient history, applicable to a different people in a different time. For background purposes, know that in Bible days women were literally the possessions of their husbands. The Jews had a low view of women, and it is within this cultural environment that Jesus came onto the scene. Jesus did more for women than any other person or movement in history. Can you find any woman in the Bible speaking against Jesus? Me, either. Somewhere along the line, women began to misuse their freedom and liberty and did not want to be under any authority, but that is not God's plan for anyone.

Enter Paul. Paul brings forth the principle of submission and says that women should recognize their husband's leadership and submit to him.

The word submit is not a harsh word. It does not mean to obey, as in the context of slaves or children. It is an attitude of love that wants to follow. It is willfully and lovingly functioning under the leadership role of the husband. You actually can be one hundred percent obedient and zero percent submissive, because it is about attitude.

Submission also does not mean inferior, or second-class citizen. Genesis 2:18 (NIV) calls the wife a helper. The word means companion or completer.

So what if we just refuse?

I believe if we refuse, we will have some problems with God. This is God's way, and we cannot be right with God and disobedient to His Word.

I also believe we will have some problems with our husband. God has created within the man the knowledge that he is supposed to lead. When he has to struggle for it, it will cause deep frustration.

And then I believe you will have problems with your children. There is a scriptural principle that says that you cannot exercise authority unless you are under authority. If a wife refuses to submit to her husband, then her children will not submit to her. For a lack of better wording, that is God's chain of command.

Lastly, I believe you will have problems with yourself. God has created in woman a desire to have someone to look to and lean on for security and stability.

So what if he really will not lead, or lead in love? Remember, we already said that we cannot control him. But we can pray for him. Let God deal with him. We do our part to lovingly submit and follow, and leave him to God.

And in case you have not married yet, here is a free piece of advice: Ask yourself before you marry him, "Am I willing to submit to the spiritual leadership of this man?" We told our girls before they married that they needed to ask themselves if this was a man they could willingly submit to.

Of course, I hope it goes without writing, but I will write it anyway: I am not talking about anything illegal or immoral. In that case, we answer to a higher authority.

Boundaries. Hopefully we all have them in our marriage and our parenting. Boundaries are for our good. God gives them for our good, not to spoil our fun.

Eddie and I have external boundaries when it comes to the opposite sex. Why? Because this world we live in is crazy, and we know the Enemy is out to steal, kill and destroy. So we have set external boundaries that he and I both can live with and are careful not to cross.

But along with external boundaries, we have to have internal boundaries. Elizabeth Elliot said, "The battleground is the mind. To pray, 'deliver us from evil,' lays on us the responsibility to struggle against the evil in our minds, for that is where trouble begins and where it must be conquered."

Internal guidelines mean we reject all wrong thoughts and feelings.

There are a lot of people who put up external boundaries with the opposite sex, but none around their hearts. It is possible to "obey" all the external rules you have put into place, but if your heart is compromised, well then, "Houston, we have a problem." Staying faithful starts in our thinking:

"Whatever is true, whatever is noble, whatever is right, whatever is pure, whatever is lovely, whatever is admirable — if anything is excellent or praiseworthy — think about such things" (Philippians 4:8, NIV).

The battle to be faithful in marriage is won or lost in your thinking long before making it to the bedroom.

It used to be unheard of that women would have affairs, but oh, the times they are a changing, and they have changed. I have probably had more women friends fall to this than Eddie has experienced with men friends. The reasons are all over the board, from lack of attention and affection to abusive husbands to too much time on their hands. There is no difference in the stats here between churchgoing Christian women and those with no church or religious affiliation at all, same as divorce stats. Just as soon as we think it cannot happen to us, we have created a crack for Satan. Women are abusing porn sites just as much as men. They travel for work and engage with lots of people. They stay at home and are bored out of their minds and find themselves desperate for attention. It is in every walk of life, every neighborhood, every church. We know couples who have gone through this, sought counsel, worked hard to get through it and have amazing marriages, but they would tell you it is the single most hurtful thing in a marriage. It destroys trust and breeds all kinds of hurt and insecurity. It is a long way back from this. And I would say the same for emotional affairs, as well — you know, where "nothing really happened," but boy, the hurt runs deep on that one, too. The connection we share physically and emotionally should be reserved for our spouse only, and nothing will cause the devil to kick back and laugh more than this, and it will give him a lifetime of stuff to use against us.

If you have worked through this, congratulations. I am so

proud of you for doing the hard work I know it takes. If you are in the middle of it or at the edge of it and even considering it, please turn and run as fast and as hard as you can. No job is worth it. No person is worth it. God will always provide a way out, but you have to take it.

Boundaries — they are extremely important, and a necessity in marriage.

Then there are habits. The definition of habit is a settled or regular tendency or practice, especially one that is hard to give up. A habit is an automatic reaction to a specific situation.

Anyone have any habits? I do. Some are good, and some not so good. The problem with our bad habits is that they sneak in and cause tension in our marriage. Would you say that you noticed them when you were dating your spouse and they did not bother you? But the minute you set up house together, they had a way of intensifying. How does that happen? We all have them, and we need to be big enough to overlook most of them. Every hill is not worth dying on. But, if they warrant change, we should also be big enough to change. So often those little habits become big habits, just like little arguments can fester into bigger arguments if we do not deal with them. Sometimes the minor things that at one time we even laughed about become major things that are not so funny anymore.

It is so easy to get lazy with our thank-you's and expressing appreciation for one another that we appear to take things, and people, for granted. No one likes to be taken for granted. Do not get lazy and neglect him. Trust me, there are others out there who are willing to pay him some attention just when he is most needing it and most vulnerable, Satan will put her right in his path. So be intentional with showing love and appreciation; talk about the habits that need to be dealt with by keeping the lines of communication open.

Same with our spiritual life. We get lazy with our quiet time in the mornings, and before long it has been a month since we read our Bible. And who knows the last time we prayed, other than "Bless me and mine today, Lord." I know there are some marriages that make it and have no love for God or His way, but they are rare. We are better off doing things by the book, following hard after the One who created love and marriage in the first place. He knows how to make it work. He knows how to fix it.

Our time at the coffee shop is coming to a close. I feel sure we have shared some laughs and tears together; maybe you have not, but I definitely have. All this has been about loving you and encouraging you. I hope you have felt that. We all struggle and we all have hurts, maybe layers of hurt. I am still striving to be the wife God has called me to be. It is so easy most days to be selfish and lazy and stay within myself. You have no clue how hard I still work at it, how often I pray for God to build my love for Eddie. I ask Him to make me more in love with him than ever. I ask Him to build my passion for my husband daily. I ask Him to erase arguments from my mind, hurtful words from my memory, and to do the same for him. I ask Him to make me the most beautiful girl in Eddie's eyes and the only one that makes his heart pound. I pray that

God continues to build my trust in him.

Building strong marriages is doing the intentional work, daily, no matter how long you have been in the game. It is more than a date night. It is more than good manners. It is more than parenting together. It is more than going to church together or paying the bills on time.

It is a fight, on our knees, daily — begging God to restore love, redeem hurts, build trust and renew passion.

First Corinthians 7:28b says, "But such people (those of us who marry) will have trouble in this life, and I am trying to spare you" (CSB). Is it worth it? I say, absolutely! But it will not be easy.

Marriage is not spending every waking moment together. It is not snuggling in bed with no need for an alarm and sleeping until we wake up each day. It is not a spotless home full of laughter and no tears. It is not lovemaking every morning and every night. Sometimes he will snore and you will get no sleep at all. Sometimes you will hog the covers or crowd his side of the bed. Sometimes doors are slammed and mean things are said or hats are thrown. The silent treatment goes into effect while dirty laundry piles high. There may be lots of blaming. Hopefully there is some tongue-biting to keep some of the harsh words in our mouth. It is cereal sometimes for dinner, but you do not care because you get to eat together. It is losing a parent or a child and clinging to one another while you cry until you think you don't have any tears left. It is having someone who believes in you and tells you everything may not be okay, but you will get through it together. He may be the one who makes you the most insane, angry and crazy, but it is because he is the one you love the most and cannot imagine living a day without.

The commitment, even when we do not feel like it, is a must — but I want all the feels, too. That does not happen every day, of course. He does have to go to work, bills have to be paid, kids are sick. Goosebumps are great. Instagram-worthy days are fabulous. But most days it is about just doing the thing — being faithful, choosing love, grace, and forgiveness.

Practical things help, girlfriends, but they do not hold a candle to prayer. We are being opposed in the spiritual realm; the forces of evil are coming against us to destroy us, and nothing makes Satan happier than strife in the home.

So hit your knees every day, keep your chin up and your face to Heaven, and your eyes on Jesus, the author and finisher of your faith, and know that He who began a good work — and your marriage is a good work — will be the One who completes it. Let's do it His way.

"So how does it happen, great love? Nobody knows. But what I can tell you is that it happens in the blink of an eye. One moment you're enjoying your life and the next you're wondering how you ever lived without them." — Hitch

and the other is really good, too! But we worked on all the other parts of our relationship during our three years of dating.

DAWN

I am so thankful to be able to say that Eddie is my best friend. I hardly remember my life without him in it. We met when I was sixteen and started dating when I was seventeen, and I dated very little before him. He has been a part of my life since I was a teenager, and all my adult life. We have both changed a lot. My goodness, I know he is glad I am not that same seventeen-year-old girl, at least emotionally. We both have grown in a lot of ways, but we have given each other room to grow and change. You can either grow together or you can grow apart, and so much of that is a choice. Perhaps all of it is. You just keep loving, keep forgiving, keep choosing one another.

With dating, so often, it is about a plus-minus column. We look at how the person measures up to our list. We go through an online site or Facebook friends list, or go on a reality show and compare different people. Maybe we just sit in a coffee shop and scope out the clientele. We look for the person we think is best for us. We have a measuring stick, so to speak, and we compare one to another. There really is nothing wrong with knowing what we want — especially some non-negotiables, such as faith and beliefs — but if we are just about who can best meet my needs or how we will look together, or anything superficial, we may find ourselves looking past what really matters. As humans, we are so prone to look only on the outside, and only according to the attractiveness we see with our eyes, when we need to focus on the heart, the character, the integrity of a person.

EDDIE

I mentioned before that when Dawn and I were dating, I kept praying and asking God if she was the one for me, if she was the one who would meet my needs, if she was the one who would be good for me in my life calling. It was not until I began praying about whether I was the one for her, if I was the one who would meet her needs, if I was the one who could better her, that I received the peace I was looking for. Too many are just about following their hearts, and yet we are not called to follow our hearts. The Bible says, "The heart is deceitful above all things, and desperately wicked: who can know it?" (Jeremiah 17:9, KJV). We have to guard our hearts. So many people just "fall in" and "fall out" of love and do not want to take any responsibility. They just live without any intentionality in their relationships.

DAWN

When our children were in middle school, their friendships were wide and shallow. As they went to high school, they narrowed somewhat. They were probably still shallow, but not quite as wide.

As we age, through college and into adulthood, our relationships and friendships may narrow even more. Hopefully, they become deeper and more meaningful, but they are probably not quite as wide. Little things seem to mean more. Spending quality time with people we sincerely care about becomes more important to us. There will always be those people who still party like they are in high school, girls who still act like they are in college, or boys who still want an inordinate amount of guy-time with their buddies, but most of our energy should be spent developing that friendship with our spouse.

Facebook has robbed us of the meaning of friendship. We absolutely cannot see the masses as intimate friends. My comfort zone has never been in the masses. It is not a safe place for any of us, really. My comfort zone, my favorite spot, is right next to Eddie. It is where I feel safe sharing my deepest thoughts, hurts, hopes and fears. It's the place where I feel that no matter what I share, I will not be judged or condemned, the place where I am the most vulnerable, the most transparent. There is no room for lies or fudging or holding back. The emotional connection that married couples share is said to be five times more important than physical intimacy. Maybe that is why emotional affairs are just as traumatic and damaging as sexual affairs. There is the betrayal of intimate thoughts and dreams being shared outside of the marriage relationship, thoughts and dreams and conversations that are to be reserved for the best of friends — the best of married friends.

Relationship expert John Gottman, professor at the University of Washington and author of *The Seven Principles for Making Marriage Work*, says, "Happy marriages are based on a deep friendship." Friendship is the core of a strong marriage. His research has shown that a high-quality friendship in a marriage is an important predictor in romantic and physical satisfaction.[13]

We have some good friends that we spent a lot of time with when our boys played ball together for years. The wife told me she thought friendship was crucial to a good marriage. "Like all friendships," she said, "it must be nurtured, which comes from conversations, shared interests, being considerate and respectful of one another." She said she knew marriage was our most important earthly friendship. And you could see it when you were with them. They enjoyed being together. She said, "At first, I would not date him because we were such good friends. I didn't want to ruin that. I am so glad he was persistent."

EDDIE

Martin Luther said, "The greatest gift of grace a man can have is a pious, God-fearing, home-loving wife, whom he can trust with all his goods, body and life itself as well as having her as the mother of his children."[14] It sounds like he knew something about a deep, intimate friendship with a spouse, what it looked like, and the importance of it. Ecclesiastes 9:7-9 says, "Go, eat your food with gladness, and drink your wine with a joyful heart, for God has already approved what you do. Always be clothed in white, and always anoint your head with oil. Enjoy life with your wife, whom you love, all the days of this meaningless life that God has given you under the sun

— all your meaningless days. For this is your lot in life and in your toilsome labor under the sun" (NIV). So much of life seems meaningless. So many days seem grueling, sometimes purposeless. If that is true, and I believe it is, who do you want to spend your days with? Who do you want to sit down and have coffee with every morning? Whose face do you want to wake up to every morning? When you come home at the end of a stressful day feeling the weight of the world on your shoulders or you are just plain exhausted, spent, who do you want to be there? Does it matter to you? Do you want it to be someone who gets you on the deepest level? Do you want it to be someone who can listen, or talk you off the ledge, or maybe just knows when you need quiet and do not want to have to explain things? That is the role of a best friend. And since so many days in a life are like that, that is why it is important to develop that friendship with your spouse.

For both men and women, seventy percent say that the determining factor in feeling satisfied with the sexual relation-ship in marriage is the quality of friendship. So guys, if you are looking for more satisfying sex, start building a better friendship with your wife. It is a safeguard against emotional adultery, as well as physical adultery.

Yes, I know, sometimes we start out as friends and we marry our best friend and somewhere along the way we get off track. I understand how the demands of marriage can strain the friendship. We go from dating and all the fun things to buying groceries and paying bills. We have children and, again, the squeaky wheel (or wheels) get the oil. We get busy on the job and we are trying to satisfy the boss and make a living for the family so they can eat and have clothes and do extracurricular activities. Financial stress happens, health issues rise to the surface, there is no longer any time for fun and no resources for play. We find ourselves anxious, and maybe during a vulnerable time Satan starts whispering in our ear how this is no longer working in our favor, that it will be easier with someone else, with anyone else. We lose sight of the beauty right in front of us, and we lose sight of what really matters and the fact that this too shall pass. Instead of focusing on what we have, we focus on what we do not have and instead of reaching deep and locking arms to fight through together, we turn our backs and start fighting against each other. Somewhere along the way we stop being friends. Real friendships — strong, lasting friendships — are built during tough times.

If we are not intentional in building these strong friendships with our spouse, the empty nest will be a very lonely place. And the marriage may not survive even that long. It is good to enjoy the kid stage together — the challenge, the victories, the failures — but the empty nest is coming. The kids will leave. Or you should hope they do. That is what we are raising them to do, to leave and live the life God has called them to live. I loved all those stages with our kids, but I really love the empty nest. I have my wife back full time. That may sound selfish, but that is the goal. But do not just try to survive and get to the empty nest. We can thrive in every season, including the empty nest, if we take care of things along the path getting there. And friendship is one of those things.

In Matthew 7, when we look at the two homes, we see that the one built on a solid foundation stood strong. The other home was built on a sandy foundation and collapsed.

If you have ever seen a skyscraper under construction, the first several weeks or months, all the workmen do is make a big hole in the ground. In order to build a skyscraper, you have to start below the surface. You have to go deep so that a foundation can be established that will support a skyscraper. Homes need solid foundations. Friendship creates a soil where things can grow.

If you want your communication skills to be better, be a better friend.

If you want your sex life to sizzle, be a better friend.

If you want to fight well, be a better friend.

If you want to end well, be a better friend.

DAWN

I have tried to think of the different things that have made my longest friendships last for so long. I am talking twenty-plus years of friendship. For most of them, it is the quality of time versus the quantity. We all know that adulting decreases the frequency of friend time, but the quality still matters. It is the friends I have been able to talk with honestly and openly — those who truly speak life into my life, who do not just tell me what I may want to hear — that have outlasted the shallow relationships. True friends tell me the truth because they love me, not to hurt me. Trust and loyalty are evident. We have common interests, laugh a lot, have fun, try some new things together, even cry together. Friendships are important. We all need them.

But Eddie is my best friend, and I am his. Why? Because, with marrieds, there are so many more opportunities for these things, and the enjoyment should be on another level. We have the utmost respect for each other, whether we agree or not. Forgiveness is swift, and saying, "I'm sorry," even when it is hard — and it is hard — must be genuine. There is no walking away from this friendship.

It is also important for Eddie and me to sit down and set goals together, talk about our dreams, and make plans with each other. We usually do that once a year in detail, but we are constantly revisiting them throughout the year. I heard someone call them in-sync meetings, those times we need to reassess and make sure we are on the same page. Date nights are helpful for that, but it is also good to reserve date nights for fun, if possible. I know with kids, sometimes we have to combine the two, but the point is that in-sync meetings are important and probably should happen often.

Best friends cheer each other on. I used to not think it mattered if I told Eddie how I thought things went on Sundays, how his message was or how it impacted me. After all, everyone else usually rushed his way to tell him those things. But he told me once that what others said paled in comparison to what I said. He knew many just said things to be nice, but I would shoot straight. Now, while that is a lot of pressure, it is also reassuring to know that my voice matters to him.

Girls, we have the opportunity to be their biggest cheerleaders. Do not take that lightly. I cheered in middle school and high school. I know it is not the most important part of the game, but it is part of it. And to your husband, you are the most important voice, the most important opinion in his ear. I have thought so many times how I have cheered for my kids, to the point of being obnoxious. I cheered for my husband when he played sports. I need to be more intentional in cheering him on even now.

Maybe surprise your husband with a standing ovation one day when he comes home. Let him know that what he does matters, and you are proud of him. He needs that. Tell him, and show him that you believe in him no matter what. Eddie knows he is my favorite preacher of all time. I try to tell him that every week in some way. Husbands never tire of hearing you brag on them, and we need to be good at bragging.

Someone once said, "A good friend knows all your best stories, but a best friend has lived them with you." Hopefully your best friend is your spouse, and you are writing some amazing stories together. True friendship lasts a lifetime.

EDDIE

There are some things, and there are probably some more that we will not touch on, that we believe are signs of the real-deal kind of friendship.

One of those, and probably of utmost importance, is trust. You cannot have any level of friendship without trust. There is the trust that says I believe you will be here for me no matter what. The trust that says I am willing to be open and vulnerable with you. The trust that refuses any and all kinds of secrets. We refuse any excuse or rationalization for secrets. It is never all right, no matter the circumstance, even if we believe the spouse will be upset or hurt. Secrets always have a way of surfacing, and then there is the feeling of betrayal and hurt, even if we try to convince the other that our aim was to protect. Trust is a must, and when it is damaged or lost it takes a lot of work to recover. Secrets about how much money was spent. Keeping the secret when a parent slips you money or a gift. Secret relationships, even if platonic, that you do not think your spouse would be comfortable with.

And this is probably a good place to go ahead and say that we should have one another's passwords for emails and social media. It is not that we do not trust each other, but it sets up an accountability for both.

I do not have a Facebook account. I can get on Dawn's Facebook, and I have a page that she manages. The reason is simple: I do not want to answer, comment or post. I just want to scroll. And since we know most of the same people, that works for us. Recently I had an old friend, a woman, but just a friend, reach out. It seemed like she wanted to catch up and go in-depth in a conversation, and even possibly meet up. When I told her that she could reach me through Dawn's Facebook, because it was not mine and she managed it, I never heard from her again. Surely I do not have to tell you of all the "reconnections" via social media that have caused harm to marriages. Keep yourself above board. No secrets allowed.

DAWN

Real friends like the real you. They do not judge you or expect perfection. They do not expect you to be like someone else or everyone else. They appreciate the qualities that make you, you. If you are consistently late, they still love you. If you talk without taking a breath, they are still willing to listen. If you are moody, hyper, opinionated or lazy, they overlook it and focus on your good qualities. Whatever it is that most people consider a deal-breaker about you, a true friend stays by your side.

EDDIE

Allowing some margin for freak-outs and high anxiety is the difference between a true friend and a fair-weather friend. When we get squeezed, what is on the inside always comes out. Sometimes, depending on the circumstances and how hard the squeeze is, what comes out can be ugly. No matter how ugly, true friends will not cut and run. They stay close. They allow the freak-out, and then they are there to help us calm down and see us through to the other side. Friends will sometimes have to talk us off the ledge and help us see that the situation is not nearly as bad as we think. They give us perspective. They help us sift through the garbage all the while helping us search for the gems. Who better to do that with us, and for us, than our spouse, our best friend?

DAWN

In those times when we lose our way a little and are not

sure which way to turn or which direction to go, friends who truly love us are willing to stick around and help us find the path. They are the ones who offer wisdom without judgment, suggestions without ultimatums — or sometimes no words at all, just a shoulder to lean on until we see more clearly. Sometimes we have no idea why we feel the way we do, and we can't make sense of anything, and we certainly can't articulate what we feel when we don't even know why we feel it, but we just need a friend to hold our hand and walk with us.

It is a great friend who will stick around in those times. I cannot tell you how many times I have been in tears when Eddie would ask me what was wrong, and I had absolutely no idea, or I couldn't articulate it. Sometimes we just need a safe place, a strong shoulder and a tender hug.

EDDIE

So often, we are our own worst enemies. We see our flaws. We berate ourselves for mistakes and choices we've made. In times like that, we need someone who believes in us and points out our abilities and successes. A good friend gives us a booster shot of confidence and helps us get our focus back. Sometimes they offer the tough love that pushes us past our pity party to put the fire back in our belly, even if it takes a good kick in the pants.

DAWN

Those are the qualities that we should possess in our friendships with our spouses. We are the ones who have to speak truth to one another when others are afraid to, or do not care enough about us to do it. Our spouse is the one who tells us when we are being rude, but they love us anyway. Sometimes we have to love one another enough to be honest, so we can be a better person. We can do that for one another when we trust one another enough to know that we are not bailing. We are there through the long haul, but we have to be that person who is willing to say the hard thing in a loving way rather than excusing behavior that is not attractive or beneficial.

Maybe a good thing to do is ask your spouse how you can be a good friend, or a better friend, to them. Loving and supporting does not mean enabling. It means loving enough to be honest so we can grow as a person, as well as in our relationship with one another.

Just like there are things that build our friendship with one another and build a strong foundation and a solid marriage, there are things that kill the friendship and relationship between spouses.

EDDIE

One of those things is selfishness. Nothing kills anything quite like selfishness. In marriage, we are called to do the exact opposite. We are called to meet the needs of our spouse, not our own. It takes determination and intentionality to fight the natural tendency to focus on self. Selflessness is key to enduring intimacy and a passionate marriage. So many of us want a friendship with our spouse, but we are selfish at our very core. We do for one another if it does not cost us time or money. We do not want to be inconvenienced, or we don't want our agenda in the marriage jeopardized. We look out for self at all cost, because, if we are honest with ourselves, self is on the throne. We love our spouse, but we are in love with ourselves. We cannot seem to get off the couch to help with the kids. We cannot get off our phone to help clean up after dinner. We refuse to cook because we would rather go out, even though we know how tired our spouse is when they get home from work. We know our spouse has not even gotten to go to the bathroom alone in days, yet we do not understand why she is upset when we are planning a weekend away with the guys for golf or hunting or fishing or whatever. Selfishness is just always thinking of ourselves first and caring very little how it will affect our spouse.

Selfishness is an equal-opportunity character fault. I have seen wives who are so caught up in themselves, who just want to continue doing all the girls' nights out, or do nothing all day to contribute to the family, but expect to be wined and dined every evening, showing no appreciation for all the husband does. I have seen husbands who are so in love with themselves that they lack any compassion for their wives, who are killing it from morning to bedtime and then are up during the night with crying babies and sick kids. And forget offering to change a diaper or take over after dinner so their wife can have thirty minutes to take a walk or have a quiet bath. Selfishness knows no gender.

DAWN

Rudeness is a friendship killer. Have you heard the way some spouses talk to one another? Not only the cruelty of the words, but the tone of voice and facial expressions are enough to make you want to — well, several things come to mind. Does anyone really want to be friends with someone who is rude and demanding? Not I. It has been said that everything we ever really needed to know we learned in kindergarten. Good manners, the way you speak to people, the way you treat people, will determine whether you have many friend-ships or not, and it will determine the depth of your friend-ship with your spouse. It does not hurt, or make you less-than, to say please and thank you, and speak kindly. You know what they say about drawing more flies with honey than vinegar? It is true.

Something that always makes me uncomfortable is when I am with a couple who starts arguing, and the argument is over nothing. I mean, it is trivial on every level. I like what I heard someone say, "If it won't matter in five years, don't spend five minutes arguing about it." Is it really that big a deal if the car-pet was red or burgundy? Does it really matter if the neighbor showed up five minutes early or eight minutes early? What does it matter if the blanket is white or cream? We laugh, but, no lie, I have heard people argue over things just as silly.

And then what about trying to deal with the one who just has to have the last word? And it is almost always a rude word. Because, once we have been going back and forth to the point that we have to have the last word, it is rarely a positive, uplifting kind of word. It is about knowing when to cut it off, when to walk away, when to tone it down.

And, a word about our phones, since we all have a tendency to display rudeness in that area. Do you know what phubbing is? It is the act of being on your cell phone instead of giving your full attention to someone when you are together. Does that hit any of us between the eyes? We have probably all been guilty of that at some point, and it is something that requires much discipline on our part.

There really is no excuse for rudeness. It is a character flaw. We want to excuse ourselves and call it a bad mood, hormones, that time of the month, whatever. But we do not get to do that. The way we talk to others and treat others says everything we all need to know about what is on the inside of us.

EDDIE

Toxicity is something that puts a huge strain on relationships. Who wants to be around a toxic person? What exactly does a toxic person look like? Ever known anyone who is super needy? The person who is never happy and always a victim? The person who is critical of everyone and everything? Nothing is ever enough for them? The one who thinks everyone should act like them, believe like them, think like them? The one who is always divisive and creates conflict in the best of circumstances? That is what it looks like. No one wants to be around that person, let alone be a friend to that person. We need to fight those tendencies, as well the selfishness and rudeness that we can all be guilty of at times. All these things are within us, and it takes effort sometimes not to give way to them. In our marriages, we tend to let our hair down, and so often when we do, these are the things that come pouring out. Our relationship with our spouse suffers, and it kills the friendship and can eventually, if gone unchecked, destroy the love.

DAWN

Building a friendship takes time and effort, and we never arrive. Yes, Eddie is my best friend. We have arrived at that. But there are so many areas that we both continue to need to work on to be the friend that each other deserves. It is a daily choice to lay down the needs we have and focus on the needs of the other. It is a daily choice to bite our tongue and not say that rude thing we think will make us feel better. It is a daily choice to see things through the eyes of the other person, rather than thinking that they are wrong if they do not feel like we feel.

Building a friendship with one another means we show physical affection that does not lead to sex — things such as hand-holding, hugging, kissing. Massaging one's neck without sex being on auto. One of my favorite things is holding Eddie's hand. It makes me feel secure, noticed, taken care of.

Building a strong marital friendship means we think on the positive qualities of our spouse and celebrate those things. Speak words of affirmation and praise to one another for the good things. Spouses need that just like children do.

Spend time together. Do some activities together that you both enjoy, or try something your spouse enjoys. We have already said that quality is important, but it can be like giving a starving person one bite of the best filet mignon — but just one bite. He is still going to starve. Quantity is also important. I am one who would rather have a little every day than one big grandiose gesture once in a while. That does not mean Eddie can take a two-hour lunch every day to spend time with me, but it does mean that we do not ignore each other all week waiting for Saturday to come so we can talk about the entire week. That just does not work for me. Find what works for you, but figure it out together.

And finally, do not let things fester. Do not sweep things under the rug. Do not make a big deal out of every little thing. But if we do not deal with little things, they will become bigger things sooner than later. Deal with it. And then move on. Working shoulder to shoulder to raise kids, serving our churches and communities, enjoying activities together, having face-to-face conversations and allowing intimacy to grow, will create a friendship that is sweet in every season of life. And nothing is better than getting to live with your very best friend.

"You and I are a team; there is nothing more important than our friendship." — Monsters, Inc.

Chapter Nine

There is life after children.

"Two weeks ago I was in the worst relationship of my life. She treated me poorly, we didn't connect. I was miserable. Now, I am in the best relationship of my life with the same woman. Love is a mystery." — The Office

D A W N

Hopefully you know me a little better now than when you started reading this book. However, there may still be a few things you do not know. For instance, you may not know, unless we have been friends for a long time, that I am one who always dreaded the empty nest. Not because the thought of life with just Eddie and me again was a bad thing. I remember well life before children, when we were actually people and not just someone's mom or dad. And it was good — extremely good. I remember taking off at a moment's notice to do something fun and spontaneous. I remember staying up late and sleeping late. I remember getaways that did not demand planning for others to be taken care of. I remember watching what we wanted to watch on television or going to see the movies we preferred before it all turned to Disney. I remember how easy it was, and how much cheaper it was, to go out to dinner.

EDDIE

Unlike Dawn, I never dreaded the empty nest. I looked forward to the day that I had my wife back full time, all to myself. That does not mean that I did not love our children. I did. I do. I enjoyed all the things of being a dad, coming home to them running to me, at least when they were young. I loved Saturdays with them, in the yard and by the pool. I loved the family vacations, and travel ball, and watching my boys and girls enjoy their sports and extracurricular activities. I loved watching my girls dance and do gymnastics and cheer as much I enjoyed watching my boys play baseball, football, and basketball. I loved the busyness, to some extent. I loved our time when we did karate classes as a family. I love even more seeing how well they have grown up, how they have chosen their spouses wisely and how they are making an impact at their jobs and in their communities. I love the adult conversations and even learning from them.

But, yes, I enjoy the empty nest. I made that comment one time in a sermon, and my daughter let me know that was rude. I think she was joking. Maybe she was. I never had any doubts or fears or dread about it at all. Having my wife to myself and the house to ourselves is good. I tell everyone we are in a great season of life. I used to travel some —my wife says, a lot — but she could rarely go with me. Someone had to stay home with the kids, and without family close by it was not easy for her to leave. Now she gets to make most of the trips with me. Bonus! Life is quieter and easier in some ways, but we are blessed that our grown children all live close by and we still get to enjoy being with them and watching them do the family thing.

Sex is still amazing. It is always better when you do not have to worry about locking the door, being quiet, someone knocking on the door or walking into the room. Actually, my wife worried more about those things than I did, but those are definitely issues with a house full of kids. I am not sure why people think sex is no longer a thing as you age. It is better when you have spent so many years with the same person and you feel comfortable and loved by them. The intimacy just grows through the years and makes everything more intimate and enjoyable. I am sure, for some, bad health enters the scene and causes issues — just another great reason to take care of yourself. I'm thankful my wife constantly keeps me focused on the benefits of good health. We will not prolong the sex talk here. We have a full chapter on that, which you can read if you are a risk-taker.

DAWN

Eddie and I were intentional all along about spending time together, prioritizing our relationship, acting like husband and wife and not just mom and dad. We put children to bed early and sent teens upstairs in the evening fairly early so we could have time alone in the evenings. We chose to do lunch dates rather than dinner dates once the children were in school, as soon as their lives got busy, making our lives busy. Life did get busy with four of them so active, and we spent the latter part of the day or evening running them to and fro and attending things that they were involved in. Our lunch dates worked well because there was no need for a babysitter, restaurant prices for lunch are more affordable, and the bonus was that we were able to enjoy the house being empty. Who would dread that kind of life? What exactly is the problem?

Well, there were several problems, at least for me.

One problem I saw coming was that I loved all the activity — not just going to their events, but also the energy in the house. Yes, some days, lots of days, I longed for quiet. In fact. I knew how much I would miss the events, the noise, the energy, the conversations. What would fill my time? Those events also provided opportunities to be with our friends who had kids involved. I would miss them in that environment.

Another problem was the need to be needed. Yes, I knew Eddie needed me, but in different ways. Kids really need you. I felt such purpose being their mom. I knew all along I was supposed to be working my way out of a job, but I was not quite ready for retirement. I had them when I was young, so I had some more good years left in me to do the mom thing. Eddie was, and will always be, priority. He knew that. Our kids knew that. But most often it is the squeaky wheel that gets the oil, and what is more squeaky than four kids? I loved being the "fix it, make everything right again" kind of mom. Eddie did not really need that from me. At least that is what I thought. The kids did.

Problem number three, my kids were fun. They made me

grayer before I wanted to be and increased my prayer life by a million times, but they were fun. They gave us a few wrinkles I would rather have lived without, from worry and a few sleepless nights wondering how it would all turn out, but they gave us very, very few problems. Girl drama, the teenage girl attitude complete with the mouthiness and eye rolling, or dating someone we were not too sure about, of course. Boys driving too fast and not always dating the girl of our choosing, yes. But parties, drugs, sex, car crashes, outright disobedience and rebellion? No. And trust me, Eddie and I take zero credit for that. It was the grace of God, alone. I think He just knew that I could not handle much and He showed us a lot of grace, more than we deserved, but we are very thankful for it. They loved their youth ministry and went on youth trips and did mission work. They stayed busy with their sports teams and were focused on that, along with keeping their grades up. They all had very good friends who were always welcome in our home, and we were comfortable with them spending time at their friends' homes. They never seemed to mind us being around, and so we were.

We did a lot of family activities. We made family vacations a priority, and dinner around the table was a necessity. We insisted they support their siblings in what they were involved in until we did not have to insist anymore; they owned it themselves. We did a lot of travel with ball and made friends out of their friends' parents. That helped a lot. You can probably tell that we were extremely involved in their lives.

We were snooping parents — or, I was a snooping parent.

We always insisted on knowing who they were with, and we had a great network with parents checking up on them. Were they perfect? No, far from it! But they were fun, most of the time. Therefore, not wanting all the fun to end was a problem for me.

However, the *numero uno* problem was my thinking that only my life was going to change. I was going to be forced into early retirement, but Eddie had years left to work. Some of that is definitely true. He still works and is extremely busy with ministry. But my mindset was that I would be floundering around, wondering what to do with all my time — and you know what they say about idle time. Yep, that was not going to work for me. I could not see that the next season could be just as exciting and purposeful as the previous one. Actually, I think I knew it in my head, but my heart was struggling. I knew I had ministry opportunities. I knew church would always keep me busy, busier than I cared to be, actually. It just was not the way I wanted to be busy.

I remember telling God one day, as I vented to Him on this subject, "I know you have great plans ahead for my children, but what about me? Where do I go from here?" Nothing that came to mind seemed enticing to me. I had quoted Jeremiah 29:11 to my kids their entire life: "For I know the plans I have for you ... plans to prosper you and not to harm you, plans to give you hope and a future" (NIV). I know that verse as well as I knew John 3:16 and as well as most husbands know the verse, "Wives, submit to your husbands." But did this apply to a mid-forties, stay-at-home mom of four when the last kid flew the coop? Yes, yes! A thousand times, YES! Not just for me, but for you, too! It is His promise for all of us.

God began to lay some things on my heart as I began to seek Him and daily remind Him of this promise. It started the summer before our fourth child left for college. I remember sitting by our pool in the backyard, alone, and thinking turned to praying, and praying turned to tears. I needed to know I had some purpose for the coming days. Everyone needs a sense of purpose, right? I think that day sent me, or us, headlong into a season not only of purpose, but of a new-found hope and sense that this could be good. Of course, if it is of God, it is always for our good. But, I confess, getting to the good would send things spiraling upside down and side-ways.

EDDIE

I remember Dawn calling me at work asking me to come home. I knew things had been off. She never called and asked me to come home. She did not do that if she was sick or if the kids were crazy, probably not even if the house had been on fire, so I knew something was up. She had been quieter than normal, and even though she internalizes things and is a deep thinker, this was more than the norm.

I went home to find her on our back porch. She began to share, a lot more in-depth, about what had been going on with her and how she was feeling. She said God had laid some things on her about the future, and, quite frankly, they were scary. I had been dealing with a lot, as well, and had internalized things so as not to add to her load. But the more we talked, the better it felt, so we talked and talked and talked. It felt good to get it all out on the back porch that day. And the more we talked, the more we realized we were on the same page and had been feeling many of the same things. It gave both of us a sense of renewal; maybe God was going to do something new and fresh as we approached this new season. But as Dawn has already alluded, it would not come the easy way, and things definitely went sideways.

We took a week away and went to a friend's cabin in the mountains. I do not know why it is so different when we go there, but God seems to peel back the layers, like an onion, when we are there, and we hear and see things so clearly. Thankfully, He had us both on the same page. He did not give us all the details that week, but He gave us enough that we knew some changes were coming for us, and we needed to be ready. We were — we thought.

DAWN

Have you ever wondered why getting to the good stuff has to be so hard? I have; I do. We had been in our place of ministry for seventeen years. Our children were raised there. We loved our home, our church, our friends. But we knew God was going to move us. We did not know why. We did not know exactly where, although He had put the same place on both of our hearts. And we did not know exactly how, although that would very quickly become apparent. Things began to happen quickly when we came down off that mountain.

What I was afraid would become a season of loneliness, boredom, zero purpose, turned into anything but! God did call us to move, to leave the place we had thought we would spend the remainder of our ministry.

Eddie resigned, not knowing for sure where we would go. But God did. And that was all we needed. We knew He had a plan, and that it was for our good and His glory, so Eddie gave the church a date that would be our last day, no matter what. Talk about scary! Also scary was that some friends scattered, some others betrayed us, a few linked arms and hung in there with us, and a few were encouraged and motivated to take some huge steps out of their comfort zone and do what God had put on their hearts to do. But the most amazing thing was that the people we knew through all the years, the ones who with every single move would climb into the car and travel to a new church, a new home, make new friends, start a new school, came through like champs.

Our kids joined in on the journey with us. Yes, they were living their own lives; at the time, one was married, one was working, and two were in college. This place had been their home for seventeen years, and they would no longer have that to go back to. I remember the sweetest evening ever was when we were in my parents' den with our children and were breaking the news to them. Some of them cried, not out of sadness, but instead for the sense of God working, and His faithfulness. We all just decided that whatever happened, God was in charge and He had this. Eddie has said over and over, and still does, "God's got it." We all got down on the floor in my parents' den that night and just prayed and wept together. And the Spirit was all over us.

EDDIE

That is what God can do when we are sold out to Him and His way of doing things. Our families are better for it. We are better for it. The move was hard. Starting over was hard. Seeing some people for how they truly were was hard. But, it is true that if you prioritize family, treat them well, love them well, raise your children well, God will always do His part. Dawn is right. Every time we made a move, our children were the only ones who got in the car and moved with us. No church member has ever done that with us; no friend has ever done that with us. Prioritize your family, only after your relationship with Jesus Himself, and you will be better for it. I know it is hard with work, ministry, commitments, the needs of others, but it will always be worth it.

I had two men in our church one time tell me that my family, especially my children, needed to see me sacrifice more. Those men had zero idea the sacrifices we all make in ministry. Dawn and I, and all four of our children, have sacrificed plenty through the years to do what we are called to do. But to sacrifice for sacrifice's sake, and so that others could feel more important than my own family, was never going to happen. And today, I am so grateful I recognized the foolishness in that philosophy.

God did move us to the area He had laid on our hearts in the cabin that week. We have been able to see the reasons for

EDDIE AND DAWN LEOPARD

that move, and we have seen God's hand over and over again. It has been good for us in many ways. I cannot tell you that I easily let go of the ministry I had. God had to pry it out of my hands and break me in many ways (including a broken shoulder) in order to prove to me that He could break me in worse ways if I did not unclench my fists and let go. I learned my lesson the hard way. I have taken those lessons with me, and it has taught me to hold all things loosely and to trust Him to always take care of us. I could pride myself on being the leader of my home, the breadwinner of my home, the one who holds it together and takes care of all of us, but that would not be true. Jesus is the one, and only one, who not only holds it all together, but holds us all together. I cannot imagine where we would be without Him.

DAWN

I guess you can take some encouragement from us that the problem of boredom and a lack of purpose in the season of the empty nest has been solved. Be encouraged, too, that even though it was hard getting to where we needed to be, God's grace was more than enough. I would not trade the lessons learned during that season for anything you could offer us.

I was wrong about my life being the only one that would change. Eddie's life changed drastically during that time. He does still work like he did, and it still consumes much of his time and focus, but God has been so good and faithful to fill my time with the purpose I thought I would lack. So many things I put on the back burner while raising four children could now come to the forefront. I am now able to travel with Eddie some instead of staying home. I spent years watching him come and go, and now I get to go, as well. Do not get me wrong. That was how we chose to do life with children at home. I have zero regrets about that. I loved being home with them, but there were times I felt left out, isolated, lonely, wishing I could go, too. We knew, Lord willing, the time would come that I could join him. Trust me, it comes much quicker than you think it will.

I was also able to help care for my mom, who suffered with Alzheimer's, and live the last five years of her life close by. I was able to be near my dad and not only help him, but enjoy time with him regularly before he joined my mom in heaven. We live close to all our children today. We say today because we take it one day at a time now, and we do not know if they will always live close to us. For now, we get to enjoy them and our grandchildren often.

I am able to focus more on writing, which God increased the vision for during those days of seeking Him. My children are all married and do not need me like they once did. I secretly hope they still do, at least a little bit. I started my business with essential oils, and I am able to help others who seek a better way of life through health and wellness and living a healthier lifestyle. All those things God taught me as a mom, as well as the love for helping and fixing and nurturing, He is continuing to use. He wastes nothing.

EDDIE

While I feel somewhat unqualified to write on marriage, I feel totally unqualified to write on this subject of finishing well. At this writing, we have been married for thirty-five years. I wanted to have many years in before writing. We have some experience. We can tell you what you should do and, even more, what not to do. But we have not finished yet. By finishing, I mean graduating to heaven — passing on; yes, dying. It is so cool to read about couples who have lived many years together and die together at a ripe old age on the same day, some just hours or minutes apart. I know the chances of that happening are slim, but how cool would that be?

If that does not happen, my dream would be to live a long and productive life, then when I am on my death bed (not in much pain, and with clarity of mind), have my family around me. I would love to be able to look at my wife with my family around me and say, "I have been faithful to you," then close my eyes and go to be with Jesus. Dawn thinks that is very selfish of me to hope to go first, but I want to still be able to say those words.

DAWN

Yes, I do think that is selfish, because I want to be the one to go first. And it is a ladies-first world the last time I checked. Or it should be.

Here is what we have tried to do, not only with our marriage, but also in our parenting. We have tried, the best we can, to think backwards. By thinking backwards, I mean try and think about how we wanted things to be in the end. Like Eddie said, he wants to be able to declare his faithfulness as a husband. So, always thinking that way, he had to live a certain way as to make that dream an eventual reality. For example, he has been very careful to put boundaries in place when it comes to other women — protective boundaries. We talked about that earlier. Whatever it looks like so you feel protected and your spouse feels loved and secure, make that a reality. Everyone's boundaries may look different. But in this world of craziness and where anyone can say anything and create doubt, boundaries have worked well for both of us. Temptation does not leave you when you leave your twenties and thirties. Satan will always be lurking, ready to sling some curveballs and throw us off our game. No one is immune from that. And we have known more couples who fail in their later years of marriage than their early years. So never think you are beyond that or that you would never do certain things. Given the right opportunity at the right time, we could all fall.

EDDIE

I am sure that most couples go into marriage wanting this same thing. We all want to finish well. Yet we are seeing more and more men and, yes, women as well, stumble before they reach the finish line. Perhaps they let their guard down. Maybe they feel they are "too old" or "too spiritual" to fall. Does something snap? Perhaps it's any or all the above. What I think it could also be is a discontentment, dissatisfaction and a disconnect with the empty nest. Oh, the empty nest, when the children are grown and gone. (And yes, I know they sometimes come back home, but we will talk about that in our book on parenting at a much later date.) But the children are gone, and the husbands and wives must reconnect. I know there should not have been a disconnect, but raising children took all your time, money and energy. You poured into your children, and well you should. The problem is that you neglected one another.

This is one of the things I feel Dawn and I got right. We have been in this empty nest for several years now, and I must say it is very good. As our little granddaughter Mackenzie would say, "It's REAL good." I know the joy of being married to my soulmate, my best friend. We enjoy being together.

There is a secret, however. The secret, and the key, is making time for one another when the nest is still full. This way, you are not starting from scratch. We always had a date night, and when children's activities or the church activities filled our calendar, we would have date lunches. (They are cheaper, by the way.) When we could, we would also get away for a night or a few days; we were blessed that Dawn's parents could keep the children occasionally. Now, as grandparents, we are happy to do the same for our children, because we love our grands and know how important it is for their mom and dad to have some couple time together. So, if you have children, yes, love them, pour into them, but do not neglect your most important earthly relationship, the one you have with your spouse.

However, you may be in the empty nest, the children are

gone, and you are having trouble reconnecting. Could I point you to the words of Jesus in Revelation 2? Yes, these are words that were spoken to the church in Ephesus, but they can apply to marriage as well. He says, in verse 4, "You have abandoned the love you had at first" (NIV). For many, the problems of the empty nest are just that. Maybe it was not on purpose, or intentional. It was just a busy, hectic time of life. The speed of life got the best of you. Raising children is time-consuming. It is exhausting. And sometimes it is even heartbreaking. It takes a lot out of you. You had nothing left for your spouse at the end of the day. Now the children are gone and there is a stranger in the house.

DAWN

I remember when my mom was really struggling with Alzheimer's. She would call me many times and talk about "this man" who would not leave the house. She was scared of him and wanted him out. That man was my dad. They had been married for over fifty years, but because of this horrible disease, she had no idea who he was. Most of the time she had no idea who I was when I would visit her. She would always ask me how my parents were doing. Sad? Extremely. It was heartbreaking that she did not know us.

But how much more heartbreaking is it to be in your right mind and married to someone and have no idea who that person is? His or her interests have changed. They have grown in different areas and their opinions have changed on subjects and you wonder who the heck they are any more. You are not even sure you want to know them.

When Eddie and I started dating, there was instant attraction. I could not get enough of him. I wanted to know what his thoughts were on every subject you could think of. I wanted to know the things that got him excited and what he was passionate about. I wanted to know what made him sad or happy or angry. I could talk to him for hours and never tire of his presence. If you could say that same thing about your early days together, but not so much anymore, go back in time. Remember, we said to think about how you want the end result to look. No one wants to live with a stranger. So go back to the time when he or she was not a stranger. Think on the things you had in common, the things that attracted you to him or her. Maybe those things have changed. Find new things. Ask God to make them stand out to you so you can connect. I promise you, that is God's desire for you, as well. Ask Him, and He will show you. He does not want you living in dread. He wants your marriage to thrive all the way to the final chapter. And with Him, it can do that.

You will not always have preschoolers in your house. They will not always be needing your time and attention. You will not always have teenagers in your house, either. They will not always be driving you crazy. Think about life when they are gone and what you want that to look like. Have some mentors in your life who are already there and killing it in that season of life. I promise you that it was not, and is not, easy for them. It is not for any of us. It means putting in the hard work right where you are today and making it happen, making it a reality in the days to come. You will be so glad that you did.

If you are in that place of being strangers to one another, there is always a way out. And I do not mean out of the marriage. I mean there is a way to find some common ground and enjoy one another again and love one another again. It starts with talking. And it only takes one of you. It is best if it is both of you, but someone has to take the lead.

EDDIE

So Jesus has the remedy. Go with me in Revelation chapter 2 to verse 5. Jesus shares the prescription, and I will sum it up in three words: Remember, repent, and repeat.

He says remember how far you have fallen. We might have to think way back. Maybe it has been a long time. But try and remember how it was when you first fell in love and got married. Remember how he or she could do no wrong. Remember how the little things were cute and unique instead of annoying and aggravating. Remember how you could not wait to be together, and when you were together, time seemed to stand still. Remember.

Then, Jesus says to repent. That means to turn away from your current path. It means to stop doing those things that pulled you apart. You should have time now, and hopefully you have the health, with God's help, to turn back the clock. Make the necessary apologies. Forgive one another. Agree together that from this day forward, things will be different. We will fight together, back-to-back instead of nose-to-nose.

And lastly, Jesus says to repeat: "Do what you did at first."

Some would say return to those pre-children days when you were so connected and so much in love. Do the things you used to do, go to the places you used to go. Find some new places and ways to enjoy one another. You can probably better afford them now. Let Jesus heal and restore your marriage.

I saw all this illustrated in real life in our own family. Dawn's mom and dad were as different as night and day. Yes, opposites often attract, but it can be more of a challenge, and it can create a very interesting environment, perhaps an extremely rocky one. I am going to let Dawn tell this story, because it is more hers than mine to tell.

DAWN

Rocky would be a good word to describe the environment. Honestly, I do not remember it always being like that. Maybe they hid it well early on. Maybe it was not always like that. But I do not remember ever sensing a problem until I was about thirteen. Maybe that is when most of us become more in tune to relationships. To say it was always a bad scene would be far from the truth. Most of the time, life was great at our house. They were amazing parents, supporting my brother and me in everything we did. They worked hard, providing all, and more, than we needed. We had fabulous family vacations. Church was always non-negotiable. We went. They served. We were raised on Christian principles and beliefs. But they struggled in getting along with one another. It is funny how we often say that the "two should become one," but some couples just cannot decide which one. I would say that that would ring true for my parents. They were just different, which was okay until there was a big issue and they saw things in two different ways. My mom had the temper. My dad always said he used to have a temper, but they could not both keep theirs or it would have been explosive.

When I was in high school and my brother was away at college, they began to really struggle. There were financial struggles, which led to relationship struggles, a never-ending cycle. Their empty nest was approaching, and I would not say that they did not know each other, which is usually the problem. They knew each other; they just no longer liked each other. That is not an assumption. I heard my mom tell my dad one Saturday morning, "I love you; I just don't like you." (We have come to see that this is a problem for many couples. Love is one thing. Like is another.)

After a few more years of problems, constant heartache and tension, my mom thought the only answer was divorce. Eddie and I had just married. My brother had just married. The time was perfect, so she thought, for them to start over — only not with each other. Against my dad's wishes, she filed, and that was that. Or so we thought.

Eddie and I had moved away after getting married. We were still close to both of them relationally, but distance prevented us from spending a lot of time with them. We were not privy to their daily routines, other than we knew they worked and were just living life.

My mom had planned on coming for a visit one weekend when she called a few days before to ask if it would be okay if

Dad came with her. After I picked myself and my phone up off the floor, I said, "Suurrre." I hung up and told Eddie, and we were both at a loss for words.

We knew they still did not like each other. I always felt like they loved each other, but there is also this desire to like the person you are married to, and that was not present. It had not been a reality for years. I can say, in all honesty, that once they divorced I never prayed for them to get back together. For years before their divorce, I prayed that they would get along, like each other, make it work. I wanted them to get back together, but I did not even feel like God could make that happen. But I am a believer that when we cannot find our way to pray for something, He still knows the desires of our heart.

They told us that weekend of all that God had been doing in their lives. They told us how God had worked on them separately and then brought them back to a place where they not only still loved each other, but they liked each other and wanted to try again. They were planning on getting remarried. And it was my mom who really wanted this.

My first thought, after coming back from what felt like the twilight zone, was "No way! This won't work, and I'm not going through it all again." And that is what I told them. They promised us that what they were experiencing was a God thing. They had been talking and praying together for months. It was not spur of the moment. God had worked a miracle in their hearts, and they knew they were supposed to reconcile.

So they did. Eddie, along with their pastor, performed a beautiful ceremony. Our oldest daughter, Chrissie, our only child at the time, was their flower girl. And the marriage I always wanted for them when I was a teenager began that day.

And it lasted for the next thirty years. Thanks be to God! He is still a miracle-working God. I remember they shared their story at church one night at the invitation of the same pastor who was part of their remarriage ceremony. He told us later that their story was the greatest story of repentance and forgiveness he had ever seen, and he has been in ministry longer than we have.

My dad told me in the days following my mom's death, how many people had told him that their story had affected them. He said some told him that their marriage was on the brink of divorce when they heard them share their story that night, and they decided to give it another shot. Some told him that they were in the middle of a divorce when they decided to stop and try again. Even others said it made them take a look at their relationship and how they were treating their spouse and the direction they were headed, and they made changes.

All because two people decided to back up, seek God, be obedient and then tell others what God had done. Even when their own family thought they had totally lost it. Even when the plan seemed ridiculous. They chose God's way and chose one another. One more time.

They remembered. They repented. And they repeated.

EDDIE

Do you see why, when married couples decide to divorce because "there's just no hope," Dawn and I cannot wrap our minds around that? Do you see why, when couples refuse to forgive and believe that God can work if they trust Him and choose to let Him, that we struggle to understand? We have lived that with those closest to us. We have seen what God can do. We know the power of forgiveness. We know that when God puts things together, or back together, it really can be better than before.

We would have believed God could reunite anyone we knew at the time more than Dawn's parents. We never thought it was possible. The bitterness, the anger, the resentment they both had coddled and nursed, was real. But God! However, it does call for two people who are sold out to God's best and God's way. It takes two people who are willing to do the hard work and have the attitude of "whatever it takes." Dawn's parents never thought they would divorce. They did not want to go against everything they had ever been taught or believed about marriage. They just got caught up in life and self and the world's ideas of happiness and success and found themselves far from God, in a pit of their own making.

That is a real possibility for all of us. But thankfully, God does not like leaving His children in pits. And thankfully, He does not expect us to get ourselves out of them on our own. And thankfully, He is in the business of bringing beauty from ashes. He turns lives around on a daily basis. He works miracles in the mundane, and He never gives up on us. We should not give up on Him, either. He truly is capable of doing more in us and through us than we could ever imagine.

I can say from experience, the empty nest is great. Dawn

and I have been blessed with good health, and I can speak for myself that the physical attraction and the sexual part of marriage is better than it has ever been. (I know I just grossed out our children.) We have more time, more resources and fewer interruptions, and we just love spending time together. We are best friends.

Now, turning sixty, I could be in the fourth quarter of my life. (I hope I am not in overtime or extra innings.) We always told our boys when they were playing ball, never walk off the field thinking you could have done more. Walk off knowing you gave it everything you had on every single play. Truth is that no one knows how much time they have left in the game of life. So, whenever the clock runs out, or that walk-off run scores, know that you gave it everything you had to give. And finish well.

Remember the prayer that we started this journey with? The very end of that prayer issues a challenge and gives us a goal, that all of us who are married would never lose the wonder and awe of married love. It goes like this:

"May they never take each other's love for granted, but always experience that wonder that exclaims, 'Out of all this world, you have chosen me!' And when life is done and the sun is setting, may they be found then, as now, hand in hand, still thanking God for each other. Amen."

And that is our prayer for each of you.

"I got gaps; you got gaps; we fill each other's gaps." — Rocky

Acknowledgments

Here is an attempt to say thank you to those along our journey who have loved us well for a long time. Some have been a part of our life as long as we have had life, and others for a season, but all are tremendously important to us and loved by us.

First to our **parents and grandparents**, who are all in heaven today: You left us with an amazing legacy that we pray we can carry on. You loved Jesus and did everything you could to point us to Him. You set the bar high on how to love Him by serving others. You taught us the importance of family and sticking together, supporting one another and loving no matter what. You did that through owning your failures and humbly pointing us to Jesus for any success we might have. We love you and look forward to being reunited. Now, if we can finish our race as well as you did yours.

To **Hugh and Doris Merck**, a second mom and dad to both of us, our first and forever life mentors in every way: You took us, a young dating couple, under your wing, lived authentically in front of us, answered all our questions and some we did not even know to ask. Thank you for loving us as though we were your own kids. You taught us that nothing is beyond God's redemptive work and that marriage is a true miracle. You taught us that it is worth the work and worth it to just hang in there most days, to keep loving, keep forgiving, keep choosing each other. We love you and cannot imagine where we would be today had God not caused our paths to cross.

To **Joe and Karen Sawyer**: You are the gold friends. The friends we have known and loved a long time. We met you when our family was still very young and incomplete. You stood with us through the tough days and the greatest and most exciting days of ministry and family. You were there at the birth of our boys, and you helped us with words and actions. You have been our example for what marriage should look like and how it truly can glorify God. You have been our mentors in every area of our lives for over thirty years. Thank you for leading the way in every way. We have followed you, as many others have, as you have followed Christ.

To the churches we have been blessed to serve:

Wakefield-Central: You took in two very young kids who had not even finished seminary to be a part of your family. You allowed Eddie to pastor with a huge learning curve. You treated us just like your own. Many of you welcomed us to your family gatherings, barbecues and Sunday lunches, and you babysat our firstborn as if she were your own grandchild, like we were your own children. You have no idea what that meant to us, being in a strange city with no family close by. We love you — always have, always will.

Bethel: We know our time there was short, but the impact was huge. It was a whirlwind there as another little girl joined our family and you showered us with so many blessings, both materially and relationally. We made friends fast with some of you, and as a church you allowed us to minister in a way that helped us learn how to balance both ministry life with a growing family. We love you and are so grateful for you.

Lee Road: We came as a family of four that quickly grew to six. We spent five of our best years there with you. We saw enormous growth of young families, and we did our share of adding to the nursery. There were families joining, buildings being built, relationships happening, lots of learning still happening, and we made a tremendous number of friends, thanks to Joe and Karen Sawyer for knowing just how to love and connect young families. What an amazing time of ministry and life we had there. We could have spent a lifetime there with you all. We love you! Please know that some of our greatest memories came from those five years with you.

Millbrook: I cannot even fathom the words to put to paper here. Seventeen years of life and ministry. Our four kids were eight and under when we rolled into town. We raised them almost through college in your midst. And you raised them with us. You were so good to us. You allowed our kids to be kids. You allowed us to prioritize family. And we are forever grateful. Nothing could be more important to us than that. Ministry there was more than we could have ever dreamed. God did some amazing things during our time with you, things that we continue to be in awe of and thankful for. Thank you for loving us well and for the freedom to minister and live life in the way God led us. You will forever own a huge piece of our hearts.

Fairview: You entered our life at a time when God had turned everything upside down. It was a good and refreshing time in our life, but a challenging and difficult time. You welcomed us and loved us with more southern hospitality than we knew what to do with. We knew long before we knew you as a church that God was calling us to this area, and He had already caused us to love a people we did not yet know. We are so thankful it was you. Your kindness and care have enabled us to embrace the stretching and the growth that God brought our way. We love you and will forever be grateful for you. Now let us continue serving the Lord together for a long time to come.

I think once you read this book you will have little doubt how important family is to us. So let us attempt to say thank you to the most important people in our lives.

Chrissie Hux: You were our guinea pig, the one God blessed us with first, so all things parenting got practiced on you first. You have made our life richer from day one with your smile, your determination, and even your strong will. I would say it has served you well, as you constantly chose Jesus, even when it was hard. But you have never chosen the easy over the difficult, the lazy over the diligent or the comfort zone over the danger zone. Your ability to know when to speak and what to say makes you a Proverbs 31 woman and an amazing pastor's wife. Young girls, especially your own three little ones, would be very wise to follow you, as you have followed Christ all your life. We could not be more proud of you or crazy about you. We love you!

Jessica Broome, our baby girl: You have always been fresh air and sunshine. Growing up, you always befriended the friendless and had a heart of gold for the hurting. And that little girl has grown up to be a young woman with the same character traits, just an even bigger heart. You have brought more joy and laughter and fun than we ever thought possible, and we thank you for that. You notice things and people, and that is such a gift in a world where people feel overlooked and invisible. You challenge us to be better, to do better. Your boys are blessed to have such a warrior mom. We could not possibly love you any more than we do!

Stephen Leopard, our first boy on the scene: It is hard to write all the emotions we feel for you. Just like your biblical namesake, you are full of power and grace. From the time you could walk and talk, you have always been about walking towards others, talking to anyone and everyone, but also listening and hearing them. No one makes others feel seen, heard, understood, and loved more than you. And thank God you got your grandfather's sense of humor. You are a gift to all, and our grace gift. We were not sure we would survive you with your boundless energy, your love for risks and your constant "What are we doing next?" outlook, but we did. We cannot wait to watch you embrace fatherhood. You're going to be a fabulous dad. We could not be more proud of you or love you any more!

John Leopard, the baby of the family, known as John

Michael, or John John, for most of your life: Dad said you were going to be our last, our omega, so I soaked up every second I could with you and it still was not enough. Thank God you were so easy, since there were three others in the house. You bring such calm to a room, to a situation, and that is a gift. When all else seems chaotic and out of control, your presence breeds peace and quiet. You are our deep thinker, slow to speak, slow to become angry, the strong, silent type. We need more of you in this world. May your tribe ever increase. Thank you for standing up for others even if you stand alone. Jaxon is more blessed than he knows to have you as his dad. We love you in the most overwhelming way that we can.

We tell everyone that all of our kids married up. We could not have chosen anyone better for each of them. They are not perfect, but they are perfect for each other. To the ones who had a choice, and still chose to be a part of this family:

Michael Hux: We will never forget meeting you for the first time, at different times. Eddie met you in a staff meeting and was blown away with your people skills, manners, and the way you knew how to make everyone in the room feel special and noticed. I met you in a student ministry worship service and stood back for a while and watched you work a room, meeting and greeting everyone with a warm smile and friendly hug. As we got to know you, our amazement continued as we saw the pure love for Jesus pour out from you and saw a heart that was motivated for everyone else to know this Jesus that you love so well. You are the best girl-dad we know. How blessed those girls are to have you! I'm not sure if Chrissie fell in love with you first or if we did, but we are thankful you have stuck around. We love you and are blessed by you every day!

Justin Broome: You are who we long to be when we grow up. You challenge us to love bigger, to act rather than talk, to give more of ourselves, and then some, to others, and look way beyond the surface of people. You are the best friend to those who are hurting, who need a shoulder or a soft place to land. We are thankful to get a front row seat to watch you follow the Spirit whichever way He blows. You are a pure-hearted worshipper, the calm in the midst of a storm, a writer of words that leave us speechless, and the one we all want around whether we are on top of the mountain or in the valley of despair. May your boys rise up and be just like you! We love you and only wish we could take credit for raising you!

Kaylin Leopard: It is hard to remember a time that you were not part of our lives. From that sweet young teen we first met to the amazing young woman you are today, you have grown in our hearts like one of our own. We always knew that you were the perfect match for Stephen. You make him a better man, a better person. You make us all better. You love people big and strong. You see needs and meet them like no one we have known before. If I could start life over, I would want to be just like you. You are the epitome of a great neighbor, a true and loyal friend, and a daughter who feels like our own blood. You are going to be a fantastic mom. This little one will do well to follow in your footsteps. We could not love our next breath any more than we love you!

Noelle Leopard, the answer we were all praying for: We met you and we all said, "Yep, she's it!" You fit in from the moment you walked down our stairs, totally at ease in your own skin, completely relaxed and unintimidated, and had to meet this entire crew. We have loved you ever since. Your heart and genuineness is refreshing and challenging. We have been blessed over and over again watching you serve tirelessly, work diligently, love constantly and speak eloquently. There is not a girl on the planet who could have swept John off his feet quite like you did, and still do. We have never seen him look at anyone like he does you. And I am convinced Jaxon will look at you the same way. You are the real deal in every way, and we could not love you any more or our hearts would burst.

And it would not be right to end without telling you that we are in love with our Gigi and Papa life and thank our children for them, as well. There was nothing that compared to raising our children — the good, the bad, and the ugly times — but now we would say that there is nothing quite like watching your own children be parents. **Brooklynn, Mackenzie** and **Addison Hux, Ezra** and **Jed Broome** and **Jaxon Leopard**, as well as all the ones that still may come, know this:

We love you more than you can even imagine. We would die a thousand deaths for you, but even more, we have chosen to live a life that would serve you well. We have tried our best to make choices that would leave you with the certainty that following Jesus is the best way to live. We have not done it perfectly. We have made mistakes along the way. We prayed for you before your parents were even born, that you would grow up to know above anything else that Jesus loves you and died for you and has an amazing plan for your life. You are blessed not only to have parents who love you and sacrifice daily for you, but aunts and uncles who do the same. Always make Jesus first, and your highs in life will be higher because of the Most High, and your lows will be bearable because He will carry you through. Prioritize family above anyone else, and they will be there for you throughout your life. No one will ever love you more than family, forgive you faster, or grace you more. Love others well. Be quick to forgive. See people the way Jesus sees them, not based on the outside, but the heart. You will serve Jesus better when you know Him better, so spend time with Him. That will never be time wasted. Jesus is everything. Now go and continue the legacy of faith.

Bibliography

1. "The National Marriage Project," 1997-2000. Rutgers University Sociology Professor David Popense.

2. Driscoll, Mark. Twitter, January 17, 2014.

3. Sermon Central. Sermon illustrations contributed by Robert Leroe July 5, 2002. "I know how it works, I built it."

4. Gottman, J.M. and R.W. Levenson, "A Two Factor Model for Predicting When a Couple will Divorce," Family Processes Journal, 2002, pgs. 83-96.

5. Barret, Deirdre. "Supernormal Stimuli," WW Norton and Co. Publishing, 2010, p. 224.

6. Harbour, Brian. Illustration from his sermon in communication.

7. Bachcom, Dr. John. Speech on communication.

8. Driscoll, Mark and Grace, "Real Marriage." Thomas Nelson, Nashville 2012, p. 13.

9. Idleman, Kyle, "AHA: The God Moment That Changes Everything," David C. Cook, 2014, p. 97.

10. Cromwell, Russell, "Acres of Diamonds," John Huber Co., Philadelphia, PA. 1890. Also in speech delivered by Cromwell over 6,000 times.

11. Lusko, Levi, "Swipe Right: Life Death Sex and Romance," Harper Collins Publishing, 2017, p. 13.

12. Eldridge, John and Staci, "Love and War," Doubleday Publishing, New York, 2009, p. 176.

13. Gottman, J.M. and Silvernan, "The 7 Principles of Making Marriage Work," 1999, p. 2.

14. Luther, Martin, "Martin Luther in Marriage and Family," Luther Works 1955-86, St. Louis, Missouri. Condordia Publishing House.

EDDIE AND DAWN LEOPARD

LEOPARD
Home Base Ministries

**Leopard Home Base Ministries
exists to help couples and families
create a foundation
that is based on biblical principles.**

Through their writing and their ministry, Eddie and Dawn share openly and honestly their journey through marriage, family life, wellness and ministry.

Eddie and Dawn believe that...

- *Marriages are meant to thrive.*
- *Families can be restored and healed.*
- *Parenting is hard, but the most rewarding job you will ever have.*
- *Physical wellness matters and is attainable at any age.*
- *Ministry is for those with tender hearts and tough skin.*
- *And faith is the foundation for abundant life.*

When Eddie and Dawn are not working, they love being with their family, traveling and just being together at their home in the country relaxing by their pool or rocking on their front porch.

CPSIA information can be obtained
at www.ICGtesting.com
Printed in the USA
JSHW041110090622
26873JS00002B/12